PREACHING
SERMONS THAT
CONNECT

Effective Communication Through Identification

▲ ▲ ▲ ▲ ▲ ▲ ▲

Craig A. Loscalzo

foreword by
David G. Buttrick

INTERVARSITY PRESS
DOWNERS GROVE, ILLINOIS 60515

124950

InterVarsity Press® is the book-publishing division of InterVarsity Christian Fellowship®, a student movement active on campus at hundreds of universities, colleges and schools of nursing in the United States of America, and a member movement of the International Fellowship of Evangelical Students. For information about local and regional activities, write Public Relations Dept., InterVarsity Christian Fellowship, 6400 Schroeder Rd., P.O. Box 7895, Madison, WI 53707-7895.

All Scripture quotations, unless otherwise indicated, are from the New Revised Standard Version Bible, copyright © 1989 by the Division of Christian Education of the National Council of the Churches of Christ in the USA and used by permission.

ISBN 0-8308-1343-8

Printed in the United States of America ∞

Library of Congress Cataloging-in-Publication Data

Loscalzo, Craig A.
    Preaching sermons that connect: effective communication through
identification/Craig A. Loscalzo.
      p.   cm.
    Includes bibliographical references.
    ISBN 0-8308-1343-8
    1. Preaching. 2. Identification (Psychology) I. Title.
BV4211.2.L675 1992
251—dc20   92-34517
                                            CIP

17	16	15	14	13	12	11	10	9	8	7	6	5	4	3	2	1
06	05	04	03	02	01	00	99	98	97	96	95	94	93	92		

To Aunchalee

Foreword

The late twentieth century seems to be a turning point. We live "between the ages." All of a sudden our well-worn ways and means of doing things seem to be up for grabs. The sciences, the arts, the humanities—are all undergoing profound revision. Evidently our cultural turbulence is not merely a matter of mild social change but a revolutionary moment—something akin to the collapse of the Greco-Roman world or the breakdown of the medieval synthesis. The language we speak is undergoing massive reconstruction; the customs to which we cling no longer seem viable; our worldview is being completely rebuilt. In such a moment, not surprisingly, preaching is also in flux.

In the thirties, forties and fifties, there were textbooks for would-be preachers. Most of them seemed to draw on nine-teenth-century classics such as John Albert Broadus's *A Treatise on the Preparation and Delivery of Sermons* (1870)—which, in turn, had been influenced by Richard Whatley's *Elements of Rhetoric* (1850)—and Phillips Brooks's *Lectures on Preaching* (1877). But then, without warning, the textbooks stopped. H. Grady Davis issued *Design for Preaching* in the late 1950s, but for nearly a decade thereafter there were few works that could claim to be complete homiletics. Perhaps the lapse had something to do with the naiveté of the biblical theology movement, which seemed to assume that the Bible, in and of itself, would provide for preaching without much help from theology or from secular rhetoric. In his *Homiletik,* Karl Barth was profoundly suspicious of rhetorical wisdom.

But suddenly, since around 1970, the field of homiletics seems to be reconceiving itself. We have seen works on "inductive preaching" and "narrative preaching," as well as other more or less eccentric attempts to reconstruct homiletic theory. What is apparent is that authors are once more recovering an ancient Christian alliance that goes back to Augustine and before: a hand-in-hand partnership between Christian preaching and rhetoric.

Rhetoric is a practical wisdom. Though we still read Aristotle's *On Rhetoric* with appreciation, in every age since Aristotle there have been rhetoricians. What a good rhetorician can do is to tell us how speakers can speak and people hear in any generation. No wonder that century after century, preachers have learned from rhetoricians. As St. Paul observes, "Faith comes from *hearing.*"

Well, Craig A. Loscalzo has written an eloquent book to help preachers preach. At the same time, he aims to renew the field of homiletics. Surely he is biblical, for he presses an incarnational analogy—Jesus Christ, God-with-us, *identifying* with common humanity; but he is also rhetorical, for he draws on the brilliant work of Kenneth Burke, a truly great modern rhetorician.

Craig Loscalzo's fine book is a plea for identification. He calls for preachers with integrity and love who can identify with the people of a parish. He hopes to shape preachers who can move beyond the "rhetoric of authority." There is genuine pastoral warmth in Loscalzo's work, an alertness to the contemporary culture, and above all an evangelical passion that is quite compelling.

Preaching Sermons That Connect is a book that will speak to preachers everywhere—for their good and for the future of the gospel. Craig Loscalzo draws together rhetoric, faith and a compassionate awareness of humanity, all in the service of God.

But any foreword is a brash intrusion; for heaven's sake turn the page and begin to read!

David G. Buttrick
The Divinity School
Vanderbilt University

Acknowledgments

So many people have contributed to my pilgrimage as a preacher that I hesitate to name some for fear of discounting the contributions of others. Nevertheless, I must recognize the seminal figures who have shaped me as a Christian and as a preacher.

Dr. Ben Bissell was the pastor of First Baptist Church in Sunrise, Florida, when we met; he was my first pastor. Ben Bissell modeled excellence in pastoral ministry, both in and out of the pulpit. His preaching spoke to me out of the depths of his journey as a Christian. His masterful use of stories and his excellent sense of humor showed me that effective preaching brings life to the pulpit and enables sermons to speak long after the preaching is finished. I am grateful to him for his encouragement and guidance while I was clarifying my call to the ministry.

I am profoundly indebted to my teacher, colleague and friend Dr. Raymond Bailey. I first met Raymond Bailey when he preached revival services in Sunrise; he was the pastor of First Baptist Church in Plantation, Florida. He preached with such warmth, care and passion that I wasn't surprised to hear later that the Southern Baptist Theological Seminary in Louisville, Kentucky, had invited him to teach preaching. When I decided to attend seminary at Southern, there was no doubt in my mind that I would take my preaching classes from him. Raymond Bailey did not disappoint me. His excitement for preaching and his firm conviction that preaching makes a difference in people's lives has immeasurably shaped my theology of preaching.

As committee chair during my doctoral studies, Raymond Bailey stretched me to broader theological and rhetorical understandings of preaching. He introduced me to the work of Kenneth Burke, whose writings in rhetoric and identification theory became the groundwork for this book. Raymond Bailey continues to be a respected colleague, whose friendship makes preaching and the teaching of preaching a joy.

I am, of course, grateful to Kenneth Burke. His personal encouragement motivated me to pursue the implications of the rhetoric of identification for preaching.

I am also appreciative of the churches I have served as pastor and interim pastor, with special thanks to Evergreen Baptist Church in Frankfort, Kentucky, the congregation of my first full-time pastorate. It was during my tenure as Evergreen's pastor that I first put into practice the ideas articulated in this book. The people of this church helped me to understand how important it is that preachers identify with their hearers.

Finally, I want to express my thanks to faculty colleagues, staff and students at the Southern Baptist Theological Seminary, whose encouragement and affirmation as partners in ministry are indispensable.

Gratia Dei.

1/What Is Identification?

Identification is "a belonging to a group of people or a becoming one with them."
DANIEL FOGARTY, *ROOTS FOR A NEW RHETORIC*

*P*reaching was not emphasized in the church of my childhood. I was an adult before I was confronted by God's truths through biblical preaching, and it overwhelmed me. The sermon was not an impersonal lecture *about* God but a relevant encounter *with* God.

During early adulthood, the formative years of my Christian experience, I matured under the leadership of several excellent pastors. They proclaimed the gospel in ways that made the message come alive. No lofty jargon spewed from their lips. In words that were clear and direct, they spoke about life as ones who were living it themselves. They identified with my hurts, joys, concerns and needs. Relevance and practical insights characterized their preaching. They preached with passion and ministered with compassion.

Sadly, my later exposure to a variety of preachers revealed that the vibrant preaching of my formative years was not the norm. Many sermons I heard were dispassionate harangues characterized by religious lingo and dated illustrations. The preachers often seemed angry with their hearers. They preached with a great sense of authority—as though *they* were the authorities—but with little compassion. Disconnected from the concerns, hurts and needs of the hearers, their sermons were boring at best and offensive at worst.

Questions kept haunting me: What was the difference between these two groups of preachers? Why did the one group seem so compassionate and the other so dispassionate? Why were some sermons so life-giving and others so lifeless?

The answer to these questions crystallized when I read Henry Mitchell's book *The Recovery of Preaching.*[1] The introductory chapter, a sermon on Ezekiel's call to be God's prophet, grabbed me like the excitement of meeting a long-lost friend. Mitchell spoke of Ezekiel's great courage to sit where his hearers sat, to feel what they felt, to experience what they experienced, to see life as they saw life. Ezekiel identified with his hearers, becoming one with them rather than standing over against them. Here was the key to the preaching that captured my attention.

The preachers who most engaged me did so because they convinced me, through their words and actions, that they cared for me. They spent time getting to know their congregations in personal and intimate ways. These preachers felt that their call to ministry was not a call to stand in high and lofty places pronouncing judgments on faces without names. Their call to ministry was a call to lead as fellow pilgrims, themselves striving to be faithful to the gospel of Jesus Christ. The preachers who most effectively challenged my attitudes and actions did so because of their words *and* actions. In them I perceived an authenticity that coaxed and moved me to listen to what they had to say. They had my best interests at heart. They preached with conviction and passion for my well-being and not for their gain. Like Ezekiel, they sat overwhelmed among their people before they preached.

I was further encouraged upon reading Kenneth Burke, a

twentieth-century literary critic and rhetorician. His theory of identification provided the method I sought. Before Ezekiel preached to the exiles at Tel Abib, he deliberately identified with them. Preachers more effectively communicate and persuade when they intentionally identify with their congregations.

Are there only certain preachers who have gifts to preach as one with their hearers? Or is it possible for any preacher to develop skills to preach this way? To the second question, my answer is, unequivocally, yes!

My aim in this book is to suggest to you, the practicing preacher, ways to identify with your specific hearers. In so doing, you will enhance the power of your preaching ministry, whether you are a parish pastor, a hospital or military chaplain or a campus minister.

There is another reason to consider preaching that identifies. Preaching that speaks to the lives of people in the oncoming years of the twenty-first century must move beyond the rhetoric of authority. People in the pews and those outside the church no longer respond favorably to an authoritarian preaching model. There are growing churches whose pastors lead with an autocratic style. But my impression is that those churches are the exception, not the norm. The downfall of several popular media preachers during the eighties created suspicions that cast a shadow on all preachers. The adage "Practice what you preach" takes on new significance in the light of these events. People become skeptical and cynical about preaching when the preacher's life does not square with his or her sermons. To expect a hearing just because you are "the preacher" is naive. Vibrant preaching comes from those who identify with their hearers, who make the biblical revelation real to their life situations. Preaching that enables the Bible's message to intersect the Monday-through-Saturday lives of people is worthy of the name Christian.

Preaching and Persuasion

Preaching is an intentional act designed to do something. My presupposition is that sermons should always have some purpose, whether to provide encouragement to a congregation, to motivate hearers to forgive someone who has wronged them, or to challenge hearers to re-evaluate their attitudes toward people who are different from them. Preaching is purposeful. Often this means that we attempt to persuade our hearers to adopt new attitudes and behaviors.

This presupposition leads to an important question: What is the relationship between preaching and persuasion? Some preachers presume that their task is merely to proclaim the gospel, to speak the truth, to herald the good news. Their high view of preaching sees it as an activity of God—that is, an act of revelation. Even Karl Barth's high view of preaching hints at such an understanding: "Preaching is 'God's own Word.' That is to say, through the activity of preaching, God himself speaks."[2] This view of preaching presumes little intentionality by the preacher. It assumes that if people know the truth, they will respond to it; the preacher's role is to tell them the truth.

But in reality, people often have to be encouraged to act upon what they know to be true. Preaching persuades hearers to act upon the revelation of God. Raymond Bailey suggests that "good preaching is both persuasion *and* revelation. We as preachers have to find the words, we have to find the images, we have to find the illustrations that will open the door for persons to see the revelation of God, experience the revelation of God."[3] God's revelation aims at changing persons—hearts, minds, spirits, behaviors; that is the premise of the Christian faith. The Bible persuades people to respond to the love of God revealed in and through Jesus Christ. Preaching as revelation and persuasion seeks to make the message of God real to people, encouraging them to respond with changes of attitudes and actions that model the good news of Jesus Christ.

The purpose of a sermon, according to the noted preacher Phillips Brooks, is the "persuading and moving" of people's souls.[4] Speaking persuasively is the task of the preacher if the goal is to lead people to decisive action. Persuading to action implies that preaching has power to move people to make life-changing decisions. Preaching invites individuals to respond to the gospel of Jesus Christ. Also, persuasive preaching calls not only for individual response but also for corporate responses from the community of faith, the church.

For example, apathetic congregations need to be called to respond to the crisis of our environment. The opening chapter of Genesis reminds us that "God saw everything that he had made, and indeed, it was very good" (Gen 1:31). Toxic waste, oil spills, air pollution and the needless destruction of rain forests have marred the goodness of creation. Humanity's creations are destroying the divine creation. One task of the biblical preacher is to remind congregations of the God-given stewardship responsibility we have to the creation.

Preaching on global issues and expecting action on the local scene means that you must provide practical suggestions for appropriate actions. A sermon on stewardship of the creation may encourage families to evaluate their habits of consumption. For example, you might challenge them to stop purchasing products that pollute the environment or to begin using only recyclable products at church fellowship meals.

Someone might charge that preaching that addresses everyday issues is not "spiritual." But was that not how Jesus made his powerful appeals—by dealing with the real-life experiences of his listeners? Jesus spoke about a man and his two sons, a woman who gave all that she had as an offering, a farmer sowing seeds, a man who was robbed and beaten and a Samaritan who came to the victim's aid. Jesus challenged his hearers to see the intersection of their faith with the reality of their everyday experiences.

The aim of preaching is to evoke a response to the gospel, a response that leads to intentional action in the lives of our hearers. Preaching requires hearers to do more than merely agree with a sermon; persuasive preaching aims at a change in behavior.

Yet people often misunderstand persuasion as manipulation, and this raises ethical questions. The ethical demands of Christian preaching require that the preacher *never* coerce or manipulate the congregation. Exploiting the hearers is never in their best interest and is antithetical to the gospel. In preaching, as in all aspects of Christian ministry, a worthy end never justifies unworthy means. Both ends and means are the concern of the gospel of Jesus Christ, if it is to remain good news. *How* we lead someone to experience salvation in Christ is of vital significance. Jesus never coerced anyone into the kingdom of God; he persuaded all who would listen that the kingdom of God was at hand.

Identification and Persuasion

What is the relationship between identification and persuasion? Identification is a means to persuade an audience. An example of identification is "the politician who, addressing an audience of farmers, says, 'I was a farm boy myself.' "[5] Here, the politician's identification with the audience is to persuade them that because he grew up on a farm, he knows what farmers experience. He understands the problems farmers face. He recognizes the hardships and joys of farming. He is not an aloof bureaucrat, separated and uninterested in the lives of the farmers, but is one of them.

Burke suggests that persons are persuaded when you talk their talk through "speech, gesture, tonality, order, image, attitude, idea," *identifying* your ways with theirs.[6] In my example, the politician talks the farmers' talk to persuade them that because he is one of them, he is the one they should elect, the one who will respond to their needs. The apostle Paul did the same thing when he identified himself as the chief among sinners (1 Tim 1:15).

There is another important aspect of identification. "If, in the opinion of a given audience, a certain kind of conduct is admirable," Burke suggests, "then a speaker might persuade the audience by using ideas and images that identify his cause with that kind of conduct."[7]

Do you remember how you felt when you were about to make a major financial commitment—buying a car or a new home? For me, sleepless nights are the norm when major financial decisions are at hand. Questions and concerns fly uninhibited into my head: Is this the best deal? Am I making the right decision? Is the interest rate correct? Is the salesperson taking me for a ride? Should I have shopped around more? You've been there. The whole decision-making process is easier if you trust the salesperson who is making the deal. If the person has persuaded you that he or she has your best interests at heart, your mind is probably at ease. When a salesperson authentically identifies with your concerns as a buyer and addresses these concerns for you, you are apt to be positively persuaded.

The same is true of preaching. Hearers come to church week after week expecting to hear "a word from the Lord." On any given Sunday morning real people leading real lives fill the pews. They bring with them the burdens of their lives: the struggle of communicating with a wayward teenager; pressures at work; the threat of a layoff; marital conflict; problems with other relationships; financial concerns; retirement; illness. Sadly, though, some people come to church expecting nothing. What they have heard from the pulpit has been so foreign to their lives that they could not identify with it. The preacher is living in a different world, immersed in fantasies, far from the pain, confusion and hard choices the people face. As they rise to go home, they go hopeless and helpless, wondering why the biblical message is so irrelevant today.

For your hearers to believe that preaching will make a difference when they face the world Monday morning, you are going to have to convince them through your words and actions, identifying your ways with theirs. All the logical arguments in the world will not persuade as effectively as the reality that you truly have identified with the lives of your hearers. Through that identification, you will persuade them that the good news of Jesus Christ does have life-changing possibilities.

Identification and Division
Identification cannot be fully understood without considering its opposite, division.[8] The tension between being alike and being different, between unity and diversity, is not a new one for theology. The apostle Paul's concern for unity, emphasizing identification within the body of Christ while also recognizing the diversity present, is an excellent biblical illustration of the ironic tension between identification and division.

If our congregations were completely unified in their attitudes and actions, wholly living the gospel, would there still be a need to preach all the sermons that we preach? Total and complete commitment to the ethical and evangelistic demands of the gospel would eliminate the need for sermons on feeding hungry people or clothing the naked or eliminating nuclear arms or sharing our faith. If your congregation's stewardship of time, money and talents were commensurate to the responsibilities set forth in the New Testament, your annual stewardship sermon would not be necessary. (For preachers who cower at the thought of having to preach about money, what a wonderful prospect that would be!)

The reality that all Christians fall short of the biblical ideal challenges us to persuade our hearers "to lead a life worthy of the calling to which you have been called" (Eph 4:1). As long as there is a difference between our profession and our practice, there is motivation for us to go into the pulpit to challenge, encourage and persuade our hearers to respond to the grace and demands of the gospel. If our churches already experienced total identification with God and the radical demands of the good news, they would already be living out the ideal of the gospel. Our preaching is needed because of the inherent gap between the church's belief and practice.

The most effective way of moving toward the ideal of unity within diversity is to eliminate *harmful* division. We do this through the process of identification. Persuasive preaching using identification emphasizes what we have in common with our hearers and minimizes our differences. That is not to say that a group's diversity is not an important part of its strength. However, we face a better chance of achieving our purpose in preaching if we focus on points of agreement rather than on places where we disagree.

Recognizing the differences that exist in a congregation is a step toward identification. Congregations are not single-minded but are a collection of individuals with different interests, knowledge, attitudes, personalities, desires and goals. Each of these differences presents the opportunity for identification through preaching.

Looking Ahead
To this point, we've been working on a basic understanding of identification for preaching. In the pages that follow, I'll develop the ideas presented here. In the next chapter, we will focus on how identification functions for the preaching task, and in chapter three we'll explore the biblical and theological rationale for preaching through identification. Chapter four deals with the preacher's character and spirituality; I want to examine how these factors affect identification. In chapter five, I will discuss the often fatally neglected topic of audience analysis. The weakness and ineffectiveness of many sermons come from

the preacher's failure to analyze the congregation—the people's contexts and their particular needs. I'll offer some practical suggestions on ways to analyze your hearers effectively. Chapter six focuses on sermon strategies that address specific needs of the congregation. We will look at examples drawn from actual sermons to suggest ways to create identification as you preach. Chapter seven gives three sample sermons with explanations of their use of identification. Chapter eight deals with specific issues related to identification and sermon delivery.

Return to the question that motivated my preaching journey: What was the difference between the two groups of preachers? The answer is obvious. The first group understood what it meant to identify with their hearers. They empathized with them, had compassion toward them, preached with passion among them and embodied the good news with them. These preachers identified their interest with the interest of their hearers because they had become *one with them.*

Summing Up

The rhetoric of identification, which Kenneth Burke describes eloquently in his writings, has marvelous implications for preaching. The sermon, more than any other form of oral discourse, has building oneness as a primary concern. Establishing *ultimate community* is the message of the gospel. Preachers can use the rhetoric of identification as a strategic method to build on the inherent diversity and unity with the church, as we sit where our hearers sit and become one with them.

2/Identification & Preaching

Having confessed to futile and perhaps even offensive attempts at effecting identification, our question is, How do we draw and hold the listeners in the bonds of identification so that the message may do its work on mind and heart?

FRED CRADDOCK, *PREACHING*

*T*he beginning point for using identification in preaching is to recognize points of identification. In any ministry setting, we have certain things in common with our hearers from the outset. In the broadest sense, having the Christian faith in common provides initial identification between preacher and congregation. The fact that you and the congregation are of the same denomination is another point of contact.

Casual conversations with members of your congregation will unearth other commonalities. You find someone from your home state, or even from your hometown. You discover that a member has similar interests in sports or hobbies—you both enjoy fishing, you have a fondness for the same novelist, you both grew up on a farm or in the city. Notice how relationships change when you find that you have something in common. The sense of strangeness is eliminated; barriers are removed. Whenever you have something in common with your hearers, you have identification with them.

Observe, however, that the identification in the above examples was strictly by happenstance—discovered by accident. For preaching, we want to make identification a deliberate act, in which you intentionally seek to identify with your congregation. When you identify with them and express this identification in your words and actions, they will hear you gladly.

Identifying with your hearers does not mean placating them, always agreeing with them, following their lead in improper behavior or preaching only what they want to hear. Nor does identification imply a false or condescending relationship with your hearers. If your congregation perceives that your attempts at identifying with them are merely maneuvers to gain a hearing for your agenda, you will quickly lose credibility.

Identification means that when you preach, you do so out of an authentic relationship, developed over time, which has distinguished you as one who is both prophet and priest with the congregation. You will intentionally consider all the consequences of your words in light of your hearers' life situations. As a compassionate and sensitive minister, you will attempt to make the truths of the Bible relevant and applicable where your hearers live, work and play. And because you took the time to become one with them, they will listen to what you have to say.

In practice, identification has several characteristics.[1] The task of establishing identification with a congregation is an *ongoing* process. Most preachers spend the first year of ministry getting to know the congregation. Once they develop a relationship with their hearers, they move on to the "important" aspects of ministry. But if they do so, they are mistakenly assuming that the congregation will never change and the preacher will never change. Nothing could be further from the truth.

In counseling parishioners, you may have heard someone say something like "We've been married for fifteen years, and she's not the girl I married!" Of course she is not the "girl" he married. She has changed. She is no longer a girl, she is a woman who has matured and developed. Likewise, if you have been at a church for any length of time, it is not the same church that called you. Even in the most stable ministry settings, change is always occurring. We all get older. Life looks one way at twenty, another way at forty and still another way at sixty. We change as we age. Families change. Children grow up, go off to college, get married, start families of their own. Communities change. Dirt paths become paved roads; two-lane streets become four-lane highways; highways become interstates. Change happens. The preacher who intends to identify with his or her hearers and speak to their changing needs through preaching must make identification a continuing process.

Assessing the changing people-pastor relationship requires you to spend time reflecting on and evaluating that relationship. Change is subtle and often goes unnoticed. It always amazes me when someone who has not seen one of my children in a while acts surprised at how much they have grown and changed: "Is this little Michael? My, he's all grown up!" Because I was seeing the changes gradually, I hardly noticed. The same danger is present in most preaching situations. Much congregational change is subtle and slow-moving, almost unnoticeable to insiders. This fact emphasizes the need for you to sit and intentionally reflect on the ongoing process of identification.

Take a church directory that is several years old, and compare it with the most recent directory. Are you shocked? It may seem like "only yesterday" that those teenagers were five-year-olds starting off to kindergarten. Looking carefully at a photo directory, you will notice the picture of a couple who have recently gone through a divorce. While the directory shows a happily smiling couple, you know how the situation has changed. You see another couple—the husband has recently died of cancer. You notice a family whose youngest daughter has just moved off to college, a single person who has just joined the military, a couple struggling with empty-nest syndrome—all sorts of changes. You may have identified with the situations shown in the older directory; now you have to work to identify with the congregation's present situations. Identification is an ongoing, never-ending endeavor.

The task of identifying with a congregation is also a *mutual* process. That means the congregation and the preacher work together, learning from and identifying with each other. Preaching does not take place in a vacuum. Effective preaching requires that we develop authentic relationships with our hearers. There should be a conversation going on between you and your congregation all the time. You are truly in a dialog with them about life, faith, hope, making sense of the past, planning for the future, helping them see the relevance of their faith in the light of their daily situations. If you are going to speak for God, and if you are going to speak, as Fred Craddock suggests, for the congregation, you must be in conversation with them.[2]

Many preachers disconnect sermons from their hearers' world because they have neglected the mutual nature of identification. The preacher who spends all week in the study, isolated from people, crafting a literary masterpiece, may wonder why the congregation does not hear or act upon the sermon. Sermons that address the day-to-day, week-to-week experiences of a congregation will be heard with great joy. The hearers know that the preacher is intentionally concerned about their lives. Preachers who early learn the wonderful discipline of listening and conversing are on the way to becoming one with their hearers.

An interesting question may be addressed at this time. How can you possibly identify with every person in the congregation, with all of his or her issues, when you have not personally experienced these things yourself? Fred Craddock suggests that preachers must learn to develop an *empathetic imagination*. He defines empathetic imagination as "the capacity to achieve a large measure of understanding of another person without having had the person's experiences."[3]

Sensitive preachers, preaching out of an identification stance, use their imaginations to develop empathy with their hearers. Try an exercise Craddock calls "What's It Like to Be?" Consider what it might be like to be a parent dealing with an out-of-control child or a laborer facing a layoff or a person facing surgery. What questions do these people ask? What feelings do they have? What are their fears and expectations? How do they deal with the ambiguities of life? How does the Christian faith address their issues?

You don't have to undergo every experience to have some sense about what is happening in people's lives. Be careful, though, that you don't assume that your perception of people's feelings is a replica of the reality they face.

Preaching based on identification is also a *growing* process. The *ongoing* characteristic of identification has to do with time; the *growing* characteristic has to do with depth. Think for a moment about the dynamics that take place when you first meet someone. Listen to the conversation: "Where are you from? How long have you been here? Do you have any children? Where did you go to school?" Opening conversations are fairly shallow. And subsequent conversations are often just as superficial: "How are you today? Terrible weather we're having. They say it's supposed to rain tomorrow."

It takes little imagination to see that if the ongoing conversations between preacher and people never progress beyond the weather and other polite but sterile topics, the depth of sermons is affected. Identification requires that the preacher and people move beyond stereotypical ordinary conversations to talk that reaches to the heart of human experiences. This form of identification can develop only over time and must be cultivated; in other words, identification is a growing process.

Mutual trust and understanding form the basis of the process. Members of a congregation will not share themselves intimately with a preacher immediately; a sense of vulnerability prevents this from happening. Over time, conversations will deepen as the level of trust between the preacher and congregation rises. Your hearers will learn to trust you as you demonstrate that you have their best interests at heart when you preach and minister. As the level of trust develops, they will begin to consider you one of them.

You can hear this process as you listen to the way they talk about you as preacher. When I was a pastor beginning a new ministry, I noticed the folks would introduce me as the new pastor: "I'd like to introduce you to *the* new pastor of our church." After a time of building relationships, however, the introductions changed: "I'd like you to meet *our* pastor." The shift from *the* pastor to *our* pastor indicated that the process of identification was under way.

As trust increases, and as you spend more time with the people—listening to them, ministering to them, showing interest in them—the level of identification will deepen. When you preach out of this deepened stance, you will be heard gladly because they are hearing you as one with them.

Identification and the Content of Preaching
In practice, identification occurs on a day-to-day basis as part of the ongoing interaction between a preacher and a congregation. You also develop identification as you preach. As pastors, you strive to create identification not only in the daily meetings with people but also while in the pulpit. Persuading your hearers through sermons that explicitly make known your identification shows you are becoming one with them. Identification deals with the way you as preacher, both in and out of the pulpit, relate to your hearers.

A study of preaching is naturally going to be concerned with sermon structure, style, gestures and the use of the voice. These elements are important factors for establishing identification. Subsequent chapters deal with the specific ways that the composition of a sermon, the arrangement of ideas, the style of language you use and vocal tonality, range, pitch and rate are crucial means for establishing identification.

But Kenneth Burke reminds us of the importance of *content* for persuasive discourse. The content of a sermon ultimately determines whether the preacher can identify with his or her hearers. The stress on substance is critical for preaching, which deals with ultimate issues.

As preachers, we believe that the content of our sermons is important; if not, we ought not preach. While it may sound audacious, our view and our hearers' view of preaching will be heightened if we believe that preaching has life-changing significance. Imagine how our sermon preparation and delivery would change if we really thought that what we said from the pulpit had the potential to change lives. Imagine how our congregations would view preaching if they believed that sermons have life-changing consequences.

Tragically, more and more churches appear to view preaching as a meaningless act. By that I mean that people do not come to church excited to hear a sermon, convinced that preaching is a transforming event. Rather, they sit and endure our preaching, feeling that being within the sound of a sermon somehow connects them to God's grace. This attitude does not look for a challenge in preaching, any more that it looks for God's presence there. The apostle Paul's declaration that "faith comes from hearing" implies a dynamic hearing experience, one that assumes that what is said is crucial.

The content of our sermons takes up the essence of the gospel and the major tenets of the Christian faith. How we handle the biblical witness, our exegesis, our theological reflection and our fidelity to the doctrines of Christianity are all critical aspects of the preaching enterprise. The content of preaching is the foundation from which all other identification strategies emerge.

Identification Strategies

Burke roots his theory of rhetoric in the notion that all language is symbolic action; that is, language uses symbols that *do something*. A newspaper editorial, a play, a novel, a song and a sermon are not merely verbal exercises without purpose. Their authors design them to create an attitude or induce an action in their readers or hearers. They have a function; their authors intend for them to accomplish something. A newspaper editorial may be written to expose corrupt political practices; a play's purpose may be to entertain; a novel may be written to arouse concern about a social problem; a song's intention may be to awaken sensitivity to beauty; and a sermon's purpose may be to evoke a spirit of forgiveness. Whatever the specific end, each of these symbolic acts has some purpose.

Burke further contends that creative and imaginative works are answers to questions raised by the situation in which the works arose. The works are strategies for dealing with the situation that confronted their authors. So Burke encourages authors to think strategically and intentionally when addressing questions posed by a situation.

Every situation you face as a preacher is loaded with questions. A child is tragically killed in a car accident. Notice the questions: Why did God do this to my child? Where is God when you need him? Why is God punishing me? What would have happened if I hadn't let her out to play today? If you are going to address this situation adequately from the pulpit, your sermon must emerge as an attempt to answer these questions. Sometimes you will do that explicitly, other times implicitly.

Summing Up

The issue is clear: preaching that is relevant, addressing the real-life needs of people, intentionally addresses the questions posed by the preaching situation. The preacher is keenly aware of the needs of his or her hearers, listening to their questions, concerns, hurts, needs, dreams and weaknesses, and strategically formulates a symbolic response. The preacher designs the sermon to evoke an action or a change of attitude in light of the biblical revelation.

Preaching, as symbolic action, participates in the revelatory action of God. Jesus Christ, the living Word, is made real in and through the preaching event.

3/God with Us

"And they shall name him Emmanuel," which means, "God is with us."

MATTHEW 1:23

*T*hroughout the history of the church, the essence of preaching's message has gone unchanged; the mode of preaching, however, is as varied as the preachers themselves. Preachers have delivered the *kerygma*—the message of good news in Jesus Christ, the possibility for meaning in this life and hope in the life to come—in a variety of brightly wrapped packages. From the homilies of the early church (based on the model of Jewish preaching in the synagogue) to the preaching of Augustine (the trained rhetorician-turned-preacher who used and encouraged the use of classical rhetoric for preaching) to the protracted sermons of Jonathan Edwards to modern messages, we see preachers using various models and techniques for effectively presenting the gospel.

Most preachers presume that a sound biblical theology undergirds the content of a sermon. But we seldom go to the Bible looking for ways to preach—that is, examining the sermon composition, delivery techniques and presuppositions of the biblical characters who preached. Raymond Bailey, in two monographs, encourages preachers to look at both the theology

and methodology of the preaching of Jesus and the apostle
Paul.[1] We can learn both content and method by studying biblical examples.

I suggest that preaching rooted in identification has parallels
in the biblical witness. With the same concern that Tom Long
has for considering form when interpreting biblical texts,[2] I
believe there is a clear theological rationale for considering the
message *and* the way we communicate the message. We can
learn something about preaching by looking at how biblical
models preached.

I must make a disclaimer here. In this book I make a case
for effective preaching through identification. Yet all preaching
that we find in the Bible does not proceed using this approach.
Notice how John the Baptist addressed a crowd in one of his
sermons: "You brood of vipers! Who warned you to flee from
the wrath to come?" (Lk 3:7). Obviously, John was not concerned with "warming the cockles of their hearts." He had no
intention of identifying with his hearers; he did not care about
becoming one with them. If anything, he created a great gap,
a division, between himself and the crowd.

Most of us would not begin a Sunday-morning sermon with
an indictment like John's. Since we generally preach in the
context of a community of faith, we are both prophet and priest
to our hearers. The presupposition of community calls for us
to decrease division and increase *koinonia* (fellowship)—a term
that Kenneth Burke would say is synonymous to identification.
In this chapter, we look at some models from Scripture who
preached out of identification with their hearers.

Moses: Not Egyptian, but Hebrew
The story of Moses is familiar to us. We heard it as children,
watched the primary department act it out in church plays and
saw Charlton Heston make Moses bigger than life on the wide
screen. What can Moses tell us about identification?

Though Pharaoh's daughter reared Moses as an Egyptian, even as her son, he identified himself with the Hebrew people. The writer of the New Testament book of Hebrews states that Moses refused to be called the son of Pharaoh's daughter, "choosing rather to share ill-treatment with the people of God than to enjoy the fleeting pleasures of sin" (Heb 11:25).

After Moses led the Israelites out of Egypt, God became extremely angry with the people for making and worshiping a molten calf, and he wanted to punish them severely. But Moses interceded for the people (Ex 32:7-14; Num 14:13-19). The text implies that Moses was not a dispassionate leader. He had truly given up his Egyptian identity; he was now pleading on the Israelites' behalf. Moses spoke to them, saying, "You have sinned a great sin. But now I will go up to the LORD; perhaps I can make atonement for your sin" (Ex 32:30).

Moses' intercession for the people, especially with his suggestion of making atonement for their sin, is an important example of identification.[3] Through his identification with the people, Moses spoke to them as one with them. Through his identification with them, Moses also spoke on their behalf.

What about identification in Moses' preaching? If one were looking for examples of Old Testament preaching, the book of Deuteronomy is a good place to begin. I characterize it as a collection of sermons preached by Moses to the Israelites. Deuteronomy opens with the following statement: "These are the words that Moses spoke to all Israel beyond the Jordan—in the wilderness" (Deut 1:1). The book contains three major addresses. Deuteronomy 1:6—4:40 contains the first sermon. The second is found in chapters 5—28, and the third in chapters 29 and 30. Examples drawn from these three addresses show how Moses created identification when he spoke.

Reviewing Hebrew History
In the three addresses, Moses used historical review to create

identification. He described the captivity in Egypt (Deut 29:2-3), the wandering of the people in the wilderness (1:6—3:29) and the giving of the Ten Commandments at Sinai (5:1-33). In essence, he said to the people, Look at all we've been through together; look at how marvelously God has guided us in the wilderness. Moses was not afraid to talk about the bad times as well as the good times, for both the bad and the good were a part of their wilderness experience together. He reviewed the past to create a sense of identification with his hearers. When he confronted them with challenging words, usually presented in the conclusion of the addresses, they were ready and willing to hear and respond. For example, having created a sense of identification with the people through a long review of their journeying in the wilderness, Moses preached a challenging word: "So now, Israel, give heed to the statutes and ordinances that I am teaching you to observe, so that you may live to enter and occupy the land that the LORD, the God of your ancestors, is giving you" (4:1). Another exhortation follows his account of the giving of the Ten Commandments (5:32-33).

Not only did Moses challenge the people, but he also spoke as their pastor. In an extremely pastoral tone, he explained the meaning and implications of the first commandment (6:1-25). This section opens with one of the most important passages for the Jewish people:

> Hear, O Israel: The LORD is our God, the LORD alone. You shall love the LORD your God with all your heart, and with all your soul, and with all your might. Keep these words that I am commanding you today in your heart. Recite them to your children and talk about them when you are at home and when you are away, when you lie down and when you rise. (6:4-7)

Again, in a summary statement, Moses claimed, "This entire commandment that I command you today you must diligently observe, so that you may live and increase, and go in and occupy the land that the LORD promised on oath to your ancestors" (8:1). In these passages, Moses identified with the people by providing them with words of encouragement and hope. He interpreted for them what it meant to be God's people: "For you are a people holy to the LORD your God; it is you the LORD has chosen out of all the peoples on earth to be his people, his treasured possession" (14:2).

Using Personal Pronouns

Throughout the three addresses, Moses created identification with the intentional use of the pronouns *we* and *us* and the possessive adjective *our*. For example: "The LORD *our* God spoke to *us* at Horeb" (Deut 1:6); "*we* journeyed back into the wilderness, in the direction of the Red Sea, as the LORD had told me" (2:1); "hear, O Israel: The LORD is *our* God, the LORD alone" (6:4).

Is the use of these pronouns accidental? Perhaps, but there are also places in these three sermons where Moses spoke in terms of *I* and *me*. I think that the use of *we*, *us* and *our* is intentional and rhetorically significant; these pronouns highlight and build the relationship between Moses and the people. As we read these sections we sense that Moses lessened the distance, the division, between himself and the Israelites. Even in places where the content of Moses' address was harsh, the people heard it because he identified with them.

According to Exodus 4:10, Moses did not feel he had any gifts for speaking. Yet we have discovered some practical ways that Moses created identification with his hearers through action and speech. He became one with them, *connected* with them. They knew that Moses was not Egyptian, but Hebrew.

Amos: The Shepherd Prophet

Amos found himself in a precarious predicament. He was a Judean shepherd, with a moonlighting job of taking care of sycamore trees, and God called him to preach.

"What's the problem?" you ask. "God seems to have a knack for calling ordinary people!" True. And Amos may have thought the same thing. "If God has called me to preach, I'll give it my best shot. After all, the other shepherds need to hear a word from God. Even the owners of the sycamore trees should be given a chance to know more about God. I will do my best to make the message clear to my Judean brothers and sisters. I think I can do that."

As you well know, that scenario is not exactly what God had in mind. God called Amos—the Judean, the shepherd, the dresser of sycamore trees—to preach to the northern Israelites, not shepherds, but aristocrats; not during a time of difficulty, but in a period of great prosperity; not to comfort the afflicted, but to afflict the comfortable. So Amos found himself in a real predicament.

Understanding His Context
Amos obviously spent time becoming familiar with the situation in which he was to preach. The northern Israelites led lives of luxurious self-indulgence (Amos 4; 6:1-7). Amos was aware of the social injustice that was prevalent in Israel and its neighbors. While the wealthy enjoyed a life of lavish comfort, they oppressed the poor and needy (2:6-7; 4:1; 5:11). There was no justice for those who could not afford it; *righteousness* was a word Israel had long forgotten (5:7, 12). The society of the northern kingdom was rampant with immorality and sexual misconduct (2:7-8). Even Israel's religion was corrupt and meaningless (4:4-5). The people celebrated feasts, not for the sake of worship, but for the sake of their pleasure (5:21). Their offerings were no longer pleasing in God's eyes, and their singing in worship was horrible noise to God's ears because their religion had lost its meaning (5:22-23). This context was the stage for Amos's preaching.

It is one thing to bring a word of hope and comfort to people when difficulties burden and oppress them. Such a word is healing balm to wounds of sorrow, grief and heartache. But to speak a word of doom in a period of prosperity—to proclaim God's judgment when life is going well, to call into question the values that are making such a time possible—is heard as sour grapes. Amos faced a monumental task, one that a prophet of noble Israelite birth and stature would have found difficult. How did the Judean shepherd and tree surgeon strive to be heard? How did he create identification with his hearers so that they would listen to his preaching?

In order to gain authority for preaching, Amos first had to build credibility. However, Amaziah, the priest of the royal sanctuary at Bethel, quickly called Amos's credibility into question: "O seer, go, flee away to the land of Judah, earn your bread there, and prophesy there; but never again prophesy at Bethel, for it is the king's sanctuary, and it is a temple of the kingdom" (7:12-13). Amaziah perceived Amos to be a threat, both to the kingdom and to his authority as the court priest. Like many others who heard Amos's preaching, the priest did not like what he heard. So he commanded Amos to go back to Judah where he belonged, and to prophesy there. You can hear Amaziah under his breath: "Who does this Judean think he is, preaching even at the temple of the kingdom?"

Amos's response is interesting: "I am no prophet, nor a prophet's son; but I am a herdsman, and a dresser of sycamore trees, and the LORD took me from following the flock, and the LORD said to me, 'Go, prophesy to my people Israel' " (7:14-15). Ironically, Amos appears to agree with Amaziah's assessment. He acknowledged that he was not a prophet or the descendant of a prophetic line. He conceded that his place was with the people of Judah, but then he pointed out that God had changed his occupation. The Lord had taken him from herding sheep and charged him with the task of a prophet. Amos did not appear to be a prophet, he was not born into a prophetic family; he was, nevertheless, a prophet. The call of God upon his life made it so.

Preaching like a Prophet

Amos identified with the prophetic tradition; he preached as Israel's prophets preached. For example, he used the prophetic formula "Thus says the LORD" to introduce the oracles against Israel's neighbors and Israel itself (1:3, 6, 9, 11; 2:1, 4, 6). Amos concluded the oracles with a similar formula that the prophets of the Lord used: "says the LORD" (1:5, 8, 15; 2:3, 11, 16; 3:15). Amos attempted to create credibility by stating that his call from God had changed his lot in life from a shepherd to a prophet. This was not a call that he had desired, but one that he could not refuse. This sense of calling identified Amos with the prophets with whom Israel already identified.

To substantiate his identification with Israel's prophetic tradition, Amos preached like a prophet. "Thus says the LORD" was his way of identifying himself not only with Israel's prophetic tradition, but also with Israel's God.

If we look at the book of Amos as a single sermon or preaching event, we detect an interesting strategy that Amos used to create identification with his hearers. Beginning with the prophetic formula "Thus says the LORD," Amos indicted one of Israel's neighbors, the Syrian capital city of Damascus: "For three transgressions of Damascus, and for four, I will not revoke the punishment" (Amos 1:3). Israel listened to Amos with pleasure because God was angry at Damascus for its ills and evil ways. Amos then moved his prophetic judgment against the city of Gaza using the same language: "Thus says the LORD: For three transgressions of Gaza, and for four, I will not revoke the punishment" (1:6). Amos then indicted Gaza for handing over exiles to Edom. Now we can imagine the Israelites sitting up in their pews. "God won't let Gaza get away with its wrongdoing," they thought.

With a driving rhythm and parallelism reminiscent of contemporary African-American preaching, Amos continued: "Thus says the LORD: For three transgressions of Tyre, and for four, I will not revoke the punishment" (1:9). He proceeded with the strategy by speaking the word of the Lord against Edom, then the Ammonites, then Moab, then Judah. Each time Amos named a new neighbor, you can almost hear "amens" from the Israelites. They felt vindicated because God was faithful to punish their neighbors and those who had committed atrocities against them.

So Israel was pleased with Amos, the shepherd prophet. He put into words what they themselves felt about those other peoples. They identified with Amos and his message: God would not let the Syrians and Edomites and Moabites get away with their sins.

Then Amos said: "Thus says the LORD: For three transgressions of Israel, and for four, I will not revoke the punishment" (2:6). The amens stopped! The smiles quickly turned to frowns. Amos had brought the entire crowd, once electrified by the sermon, to utter silence. As they cheered God's indictment of their neighbors, they had virtually indicted themselves.

Amos knew he could not come out and immediately point his finger at Israel. They never would have listened to the criticisms of a Judean shepherd. To be heard, Amos identified with the Israelites' anger over the atrocities committed by its neighbors. Then, and only then, did he have any chance of getting them to hear God's word about the evils present in their own land.

Ezekiel: Among a Devastated People

A hostile army rolls viciously into your town, ravaging everything in its path. Everything important to you is destroyed—your neighborhood, your church, your children's school, the park where you picnic and feed the squirrels, even your home. The soldiers gather you and your family and neighbors and load you onto buses. Frightened children cry as they are yanked away from their parents. Horrified mothers scream, petrified fathers are in shock; the world that they had built for their families is vanishing before their eyes.

You and your loved ones are taken to a strange place, far from everything that is important to you, far from everything you have worked for, far from all you consider dear. Frightened, heartbroken, confused, no longer in control of your destiny, you are haunted by dreams about what the future might have been.

Your captivity turns from hours into days, from days into weeks, from weeks into months. You begin to lose all hope of ever being rescued, ever going back home. The place you loved becomes an ever more distant memory as each new day drags by.

The above scene seems surreal, too far-fetched to be true. Our imaginations have trouble picturing the devastation described because it seems too extreme. Yet we know that is exactly what happened to Judah in 597 B.C.

King Nebuchadnezzar's army ravaged Judah from about 597 B.C., when the first exiles were taken to Babylon, to 582 B.C., when the temple and the walls of the city of Jerusalem were destroyed. The Babylonians obliterated everything the people of Jerusalem had worked for. The Jews were uprooted from their homeland, their jobs and all that was precious to them, and carried heartlessly into exile. They felt abandoned, even by God. Jerusalem, including the center of their worship, the temple with the Holy of Holies, the very dwelling place of God, was in ruins. What were they to do? How would they survive? How could they make any sense of their situation?

The cry of the psalmist vividly portrays the agony of their circumstances:

By the rivers of Babylon—
   there we sat down and there we wept

when we remembered Zion.
On the willows there
    we hung up our harps.
For there our captors
    asked us for songs,
and our tormentors asked for mirth, saying,
    "Sing us one of the songs of Zion!"

How could we sing the LORD's song
    in a foreign land?
If I forget you, O Jerusalem,
    let my right hand wither!
Let my tongue cling to the roof of my mouth,
    if I do not remember you,
if I do not set Jerusalem
    above my highest joy.

Remember, O LORD, against the Edomites
    the day of Jerusalem's fall,
how they said, "Tear it down! Tear it down!
    Down to its foundations!"
O daughter Babylon, you devastator!
    Happy shall they be who pay you back
    what you have done to us!
Happy shall they be who take your little ones
    and dash them against the rock! (Ps 137)

This psalm voices the utter pain and pathos of the Babylonian exile. As they weep by the rivers of Babylon, the exiles' only faint hope is their remembrance of Jerusalem. They cannot sing the joyful songs of Zion in this strange land, though their captors taunt them to do so. They even pray that they will be physically accursed if they ever forget Jerusalem. The psalmist's curse of Edom, for helping the Babylonians ransack Jerusalem, reveals their anger and hate. The final words of the psalm call for the dashing of Babylonian babies against rocks. This painful cry, difficult to reconcile by any New Testament standards of faith, shows the depth of the agony the exiles experienced.

Into this devastation and pain walked Ezekiel, the young priest from Jerusalem. You can hear the cynicism of the exiles: "Just what we need, a priest, and one right out of seminary. You know how they are, heavy on ideals, not in touch with reality, full of book theology. What can he possibly say to us?"

Sitting with the Exiles

The easy response for Ezekiel would have been to assume that he knew exactly what the exiles needed to hear. After all, his training as a priest gave him the "theological insight" needed for situations like this! But Ezekiel did not become the minister with easy answers to offer the people. He did not act as though he understood their situation. Ezekiel was reluctant to be a prophet to them, because his experience did not enable him to speak effectively to their pain.

In the midst of this difficult situation Ezekiel did an amazing thing. He sat among the exiles before he spoke. He lived with them, he learned about who they were, what they were feeling, what they had been through. The text says, "I sat there among them, stunned, for seven days" (Ezek 3:15). Rather than beginning his ministry with the trite expression "I know what you're going through," Ezekiel spent time not only getting to know his hearers, but experiencing their situation for himself.

His identification with the exiles was not immediate. As we discovered in chapter two, identification is an ongoing process, one that takes time; it requires more than an initial encounter.

Henry Mitchell's sermon "To Sit Where They Sit" beautifully and powerfully portrays Ezekiel's ministry to the exiles. Mitchell notes that even after Ezekiel's first attempt at identification nobody listened to him. His initial encounter with the exiles is reported in Ezekiel 3; not until chapter 33, well after Ezekiel authentically identified with the exiles and sat where they sat, did the people come and listen: "Come and hear; this man has something to say that matches our needs. Come and hear this man; he has something to say that relates to us, that we can understand, something that will help us."[4]

Preaching as Prophet and Priest

Ezekiel's early preaching was hard to hear because he spoke of the destruction of Jerusalem (Ezek 4:1—5:17). The people knew that the prophet's words, spoken on God's behalf, set the events of which he spoke into action. The message was difficult and painful to hear. Though he was speaking as one with them, his words were not always accepted and acted upon. Yet as Ezekiel's priestly and prophetic ministry continued, his words of affliction turned to words of comfort; his words of destruction became words of hope (33:1—39:29), epitomized in the familiar scene of the valley of dry bones (37:1-14). Here Ezekiel is given an image of Israel's restoration in the powerful vision of dry bones reconnected and then brought to life through the in-breathing of the Spirit of God. Just as God gave breath to the man in Genesis 2:7, "and the man became a living being," God's Spirit will give new life to the exiles. What a word of hope to the hopeless, and comfort to the comfortless.

Ezekiel identified with his hearers. He connected with them—physically, emotionally and spiritually. Then when he preached, they heard him, not only as a prophet but also as their priest.

Paul: A Hebrew of Hebrews

Paul the preacher worked hard at identifying with his hearers. We often think of Paul as the apostle to the Gentiles, but actually he was an ardent preacher to Jews first. On the missionary journeys, when he came to a new city, he always went to the synagogue to preach.

Paul's preaching to the Jews was characterized by identification. His letter to the Philippian church is a good example. Paul noted that he was "circumcised on the eighth day, a member of the people of Israel, of the tribe of Benjamin, a Hebrew born of Hebrews; as to the law, a Pharisee; as to zeal, a persecutor of the church; as to righteousness under the law, blameless" (Phil 3:5-6). He made a similar claim in Romans: "I ask, then, has God rejected his people? By no means! I myself am an Israelite, a descendant of Abraham, a member of the tribe of Benjamin" (Rom 11:1).

Intentional Identification

A popular way to begin a letter was with a salutation, often followed by a thanksgiving or word on behalf of the recipients. Paul used this literary form to create identification with his readers. Notice the intimacy he created in the opening section of the Philippian letter:

> I thank my God every time I remember you, constantly praying with joy in every one of my prayers for all of you, because of your sharing in the gospel from the first day until now. I am confident of this, that the one who began a good work among you will bring it to completion by the day of Jesus Christ. It is right for me to think this way about all of you, because you hold me in your heart, for all of you share in God's grace with me, both in my imprisonment and in the defense and confirmation of the gospel. (Phil 1:3-7)

Paul tells his readers that every time he remembers them he gives thanks to God. He creates identification by commending them for "sharing" in the gospel with him; this partnership brings him much joy. He later affirms that they share in God's grace with him and hold him in their hearts.

These statements created strong identification between Paul and his readers. Paul also used prayer and thanksgiving to develop identification with his readers (see, for example, Rom

1:8-15; 1 Cor 1:4-9; Eph 1:15-23; Col 1:3-14).

We find clear examples of identification in two of Paul's sermons contained in the book of Acts. The first appears in Acts 13:16-41. The overall context is Paul's first missionary journey with Barnabas; the immediate scene is the sabbath day in Antioch of Pisidia. After the Scriptures were read, the synagogue leaders asked Paul and his companions whether they had a word for the people. Paul stood up and began to speak: "You Israelites, and others who fear God, listen. The God of this people Israel chose our ancestors and made the people great during their stay in the land of Egypt, and with uplifted arm he led them out of it."

Paul was speaking to Jews, so he identified with them by showing that he was one of them: "our ancestors." He then rehearsed the great historical events of Israel's faith—as Moses did—to gain their interest and attention. He reminded them how God had delivered them from Egypt. He recalled Israel's conquest of the Promised Land (v. 19). The sermon reminded the people of the time of the judges; the first prophet, Samuel; Saul, their first king; and David, the king of the messianic line (vv. 20-22). Paul showed that he knew their history because he, too, was a Jew.

After he identified with them, Paul moved to the core of his message:

Of this man's [David's] posterity God has brought to Israel a Savior, Jesus, as he promised; before his coming John had already proclaimed a baptism of repentance to all the people of Israel. And as John was finishing his work, he said, "What do you suppose that I am? I am not he. No, but one is coming after me; I am not worthy to untie the thong of the sandals on his feet." (vv. 23-25)

Throughout the balance of the sermon, Paul demonstrated that Jesus was the fulfillment of the promises made by God to the people of Israel.

The Jewish allusions are strong because of Paul's awareness that his audience was Jewish. "My brothers," he said, "you descendants of Abraham's family, and others who fear God, to us the message of this salvation has been sent" (v. 26). Paul argued that those who were responsible for Jesus' death had not understood the Scriptures that they read every sabbath, and he implied that those who heard the Scriptures on this sabbath should not make the same mistake. He continued: "And we bring you the good news that what God promised to our ancestors he has fulfilled for us, their children, by raising Jesus; as also it is written in the second psalm" (vv. 32-33). Notice here how Paul overtly identified with his hearers: "promised to *our ancestors*" and "has fulfilled *for us*." The entire sermon is dedicated and addressed to those who would understand the Scriptures of the Old Testament. Paul, a Jew, preached a Jewish sermon to a Jewish audience.

Different Audience, Different Strategies

Contrast the Jewishness of the above sermon to Paul's sermon at the Areopagus in Acts 17:22-31. I have included the entire text of the sermon so that you get a feel for its movement and thought:

Athenians, I see how extremely religious you are in every way. For as I went through the city and looked carefully at the objects of your worship, I found among them an altar with the inscription, "To an unknown god." What therefore you worship as unknown, this I proclaim to you. The God who made the world and everything in it, he who is Lord of heaven and earth, does not live in shrines made by human hands, nor is he served by human hands, as though he needed anything, since he himself gives to all mortals life and breath and all things. From one ancestor he made all nations to inhabit the whole earth, and he allotted the times of their existence and the boundaries of the places where they would live, so that they would search for God and perhaps grope for him and find him—though indeed he is not far from each one of us. For "In him we live and move and have our being"; as even some of your own poets have said, "For we too are his offspring."

Since we are God's offspring, we ought not to think that the deity is like gold, or silver, or stone, an image formed by the art and imagination of mortals. While God has overlooked the times of human ignorance, now he commands all people everywhere to repent, because he has fixed a day on which he will have the world judged in righteousness by a man whom he has appointed, and of this he has given assurance to all by raising him from the dead.

When we compare this sermon to the one in Acts 13, we notice Paul's skill as a preacher. Paul knew that if he was to gain a hearing from members of the Areopagus—learned scholars and philosophers of Athens—he would have to adopt a different identification strategy from the one he used when he was preaching to Jews.

Paul begins this sermon by remarking how religious the Athenians were. Allusions to the history of Israel and the movements of God in that history are markedly absent from this sermon. Instead, Paul speaks to the Athenian philosophers at the point of their understanding. He mentions the altar dedicated to an unknown god, and suggests that he is proclaiming to them what they only worship as unknown. Then he speaks to them not about the God of Israel, but about the God who made the world and everything in it. He argues that the God he proclaims does not live in shrines created by human hands. And God does not require service from humans—unlike the shrines within their temples, which require human maintenance to keep them from deteriorating. Paul contends that he is proclaiming the God who gives life and breath.

In verse 28, Paul brilliantly cites the Athenians' own poets to substantiate his argument. Here he creates strong identification with the members of the Areopagus. They may have been quite surprised, but surely he pleased them because he had taken time to learn something that they considered important.

In verse 29, Paul picks up on the poet's idea of offspring and suggests that since people are God's offspring, God is not to be thought of in impersonal ways. Gold and stone—things that can be formed by human skill into a god-image—are not the substance of God. God is personal.

By dealing with ideas familiar to the Greek philosophers, Paul identifies with his hearers. He presents the crux of his message only after he creates identification. The God Paul proclaims, the same God that they worship as "unknown," demands repentance. Everyone in the entire world will be judged by the One appointed by God, because God has raised him from the dead.

Paul never mentions Jesus by name in the sermon. He knows that at this point these philosophers will not accept that God appointed a Jewish man to judge the world.

The letters that Paul wrote and the two sermons from the book of Acts are excellent examples of identification in practice. Paul had a rich sensitivity toward his hearers. He knew what they understood, and his preaching moved from that understanding. Paul was keenly aware of his hearers' point of view. When he preached to Jews, he was Jewish; when he preached to Greek philosophers, he was philosophical. His own statement that he was all things to all people certainly expresses this identification.

Jesus: Eating with Tax Collectors

The complaint that Jesus ate with tax collectors and sinners (Mk 2:16) is perhaps the clearest indication that he identified with those who most needed and desired his ministry. In fact, Jesus answered the charge by saying, "Those who are well have no need of a physician, but those who are sick; I have come to call not the righteous but sinners" (Mk 2:17).

It was religious suicide for a rabbi, a teacher, to defile himself by eating with those whom the religious establishment labeled as unclean. Yet Jesus would not allow his ministry to be limited by the whims and narrow-mindedness of the religious leaders of Israel. He did not treat tax collectors and sinners as outcasts but as people who desperately needed the ministry that he understood was his. He knew that his message would have the greatest impact if he began by living the message with them, identifying with them, feeling their loneliness and pain and speaking to them out of that identification.

A People Person
Jesus' ministry was characterized by a concern for social outcasts, those who were hated by most people. The story of Zacchaeus is a good example (Lk 19:1-10). Luke describes Zacchaeus as a chief tax collector who was quite rich. Having heard that Jesus was passing through Jericho, Zacchaeus wanted to get a look at him. Being short in stature, he climbed a sycamore tree to gain a vantage point. You know the rest of the story.

That Jesus would go to Zacchaeus's house does not surprise us. In fact, we knew he would. But remember, the crowd who saw what had happened grumbled: "He has gone to be the guest of one who is a sinner" (Lk 19:7).

Jesus was not afraid to be seen with anyone. John's Gospel records Jesus' conversation with a Samaritan woman at Jacob's well in Samaria. The woman herself was puzzled by Jesus' request for a drink of water: "How is it that you, a Jew, ask a drink of me, a woman of Samaria?" (Jn 4:9). She knew that no law-abiding Jewish man would speak to a woman he didn't know, and a Samaritan woman at that. But Jesus would not allow religious and cultural stereotypes to prevent him from fulfilling his ministry.

Again, Jesus gladly accepted the invitation of Martha to her home. He did not prevent Mary, Martha's sister, from sitting at his feet, listening to what he had to say. In fact, he chided Martha a bit for not paying attention, as Mary had, to important things (Lk 10:38-42).

Jesus enjoyed being with all kinds of people. Men, women, children, beggars, the lame, lepers—he identified with them all.

Jesus' Identification with People

According to Luke's Gospel, Jesus began his public ministry with a sermon in the synagogue in Nazareth. Luke tells us that it was Jesus' custom to go to the synagogue on the sabbath day. When he stood up to read, the scroll of the prophet Isaiah was handed to him:

He unrolled the scroll and found the place where it was written:

"The Spirit of the Lord is upon me,
    because he has anointed me
    to bring good news to the poor.
He has sent me to proclaim release to the captives
    and recovery of sight to the blind,
    to let the oppressed go free,
to proclaim the year of the Lord's favor." (Lk 4:17-19)

Jesus went on to say, "Today this scripture has been fulfilled in your hearing" (Lk 4:21).

In this inaugural sermon, Jesus identified himself with the one about whom Isaiah prophesied. He showed where he would locate his ministry: he identified with the poor, the oppressed and the blind, both physically and spiritually. Jesus understood his ministry as a fulfillment of the prophetic words of Isaiah; he was to identify with those whom the world had forgotten.

The longest and best known of Jesus' sermons is the "Sermon on the Mount" (Mt 5:1—7:29). Jesus began this sermon

with a series of nine blessings, commonly called "the Beati-
tudes." As was typical of Jesus, he used a crucial identification
strategy: beginning where he sensed the people were. "Blessed
are the poor in spirit, those who mourn, the meek, those
who hunger and thirst for righteousness, the merciful, the
pure in heart, the peacemakers, those persecuted for righteousness' sake." As the people heard these words, they knew they
were listening to someone who was sensitive and caring, one
who had a word for them, one who had their best interests at
heart.

Following the blessings, Jesus spoke of religious ideas in ways
that the people would understand: "You are the salt of the
earth"; "You are the light of the world." He did not confuse
them with theological jargon; he spoke in terms of things familiar to them. Jesus spoke to them about concerns for living.
He taught them about the importance of rightly understanding
the Scriptures. He spoke to them about handling their anger,
about adultery and divorce and love for their enemies. The
entire sermon is replete with practical guidance, rooted in
depths of the understanding about the nature of God and God's
relationship with people.

When Jesus finished the sermon, the crowds were astounded
at his teachings, "for he taught them as one having authority,
and not as their scribes" (Mt 7:29). The power of Jesus' message
was rooted not in an authoritarian manner, but in identification.

The words of the Sermon on the Mount are not easy to live
by. The people did not leave that day with a false optimism
offered by a Pollyanna-ish preacher. The message was tough,
not easy to hear, difficult to put into practice; but they sensed
that Jesus' sermon had an authenticity that was lacking in the
preaching they usually heard. They sensed that Jesus lived out
the words of his sermon as much as he expected them to live
them out. Jesus identified with them.

Jesus' Strategies for Identification

Jesus' strategies for identification are easy to recognize. His preaching dealt with the familiar; he spoke about things that interested his hearers; he made the ordinary extraordinary. The parables Jesus told exemplify these aspects of identification. He spoke of everyday objects and concerns: a lamp and a basket (Mt 5:14-15); a cloak (Mt 9:16); wine and wineskins (Mt 9:17); a lost sheep (Lk 15:4-7); a lost coin (Lk 15:8-10); a lost son (Lk 15:11-32).

Jesus spoke in terms of what the people knew and experienced. He identified with them as one of them—a son of David, a carpenter from Nazareth. He identified with them by the examples he chose, by the way he illustrated his preaching, by the way his preaching intersected the daily experiences of his hearers.

In his preaching and ministry, Jesus identified with those who had been forgotten by the religious system and the establishment. He identified with them through the words he taught and the way he lived. He preached without pretense and without the trappings of the religious elite. He spoke about things that mattered to people. He dealt with what touched their daily lives.

The old adage says, "Actions speak louder than words." Jesus preached with his words and actions. He identified with his hearers; he ate with tax collectors and sinners.

Emmanuel: God with Us

Finally, the quintessential model of identification is the Incarnation, God's taking on flesh and experiencing humanity. In the Incarnation, God completely and totally identified with humanity by becoming human.

I don't need to present an exhaustive theology to show that the Incarnation is the ultimate paradigm of identification. In God's wisdom, which so often appears to us as mystery, God chose to experience humanity fully. The Incarnation reminds us that God is not a distant landlord, uninterested in the creation and its inhabitants. God deeply loves humanity. To show this profound love, God chose to identify personally with the lives of men and women by becoming human.

The first part of the Christologic hymn of Philippians describes a view of the Incarnation:

> though he [Jesus] was in the form of God,
>   [he] did not regard equality with God
>   as something to be exploited,
> but emptied himself,
>   taking the form of a slave,
>   being born in human likeness.
> And being found in human form,
>   he humbled himself
>   and became obedient to the point of death—
>   even death on a cross. (Phil 2:6-8)

To comprehend completely the issues faced by real people, God became human in Christ. He experienced all the realities of humankind—joy, hardship, temptation, fun, pain, anxiety, exuberance, the desire to be obedient to God the Father. Paul portrayed the Incarnation when he wrote, "In Christ God was reconciling the world to himself" (2 Cor 5:19). In Christ, God identified with us.

The prologue of John's Gospel paints a portrait that helps us to understand the Incarnation as identification:

> In the beginning was the Word, and the Word was with God, and the Word was God. He was in the beginning with God. All things came into being through him, and without him not one thing came into being. What has come into being in him was life, and the life was the light of all people. . . . And the Word became flesh and lived among us, and we have seen his glory, the glory as of a father's only son, full of grace and truth. (Jn 1:1-4, 14)

John proclaimed that the God of creation became flesh and lived among real people leading real lives. In Christ's birth, life, death and resurrection, we see God identifying with us.

God's identifying with our joys and happiness is easy to understand. But the miracle of the Incarnation is that God completely identified with what it means to be fully human. For example, we know that temptation is a real part of human existence. Matthew 4:1-11 describes the temptation of Jesus in the wilderness. The temptation of Christ was real; he demonstrated his identification with us in the wilderness. Being fully human means experiencing the pain of loneliness, the horror of abandonment, the reality of death. In Christ, God experienced what it means to be human.

I once heard the story of a Midwestern family whose home was nearly destroyed by a tornado. From that point on, the little daughter of the family became terribly frightened every time the sky darkened and storm winds began to blow.

One evening, a terrible thunderstorm developed. The torrent of rain, the loud thunder, the cracking of lightning frightened the girl; she thought a tornado was approaching. When her bedtime came, she was afraid to go upstairs. Her parents took her and tucked her in. Back in the living room, they could hear her crying, so the father went up to see whether he could calm her fears.

"There's no reason to cry. It's only a thunderstorm. It will soon be over. Now there's no reason for you to be scared or afraid."

To this the little girl responded, "Yeah, Daddy, but you don't know what it's like to be little!"

Sometimes when I face difficulties or hard decisions, I want to pray, "Oh God, you just don't know what it's like to have to make the decisions we have to make, to have to deal with the people we have to deal with." In such moments, I am reminded of the Incarnation. I can almost hear God say, "Yes I do. I know what it's like to be human. And because I do, I know what you're going through."

Summing Up
The Incarnation is God's marvelous mystery of becoming one with us. The Christian faith views the Incarnation as the pivotal point of history. Divine wisdom dictated that to understand humanity fully, God had to become human. Perhaps that says to us that proclaiming the gospel completely and authentically to our listeners means becoming one with them. When we identify with them, we follow the model of Christ.

4/Taking Stock of Yourself

The speaker draws on identification of interests
to establish rapport between himself and the audience.
KENNETH BURKE, *A RHETORIC OF MOTIVES*

*P*hillips Brooks defined preaching as the bringing of "truth through personality."[1] Notice how this definition draws us back to the Incarnation as a model for preaching through identification. The doctrine of the Incarnation teaches that Jesus Christ was fully human and fully divine. In preaching, we bring truth rooted in the revelation of God; therefore, preaching has a divine or transcendent side. Through our humanity, our personalities, we proclaim that truth.

In the preaching event there is both transcendence—God's activity—and humanness—the use of our personalities and skills to proclaim the gospel. While often God acts *in spite of* our preaching, here I want to consider the role that we as preachers play in the preaching event. Becoming one with our hearers requires a look at our personhood as *preachers*.

Perceptions Affect Reality
Who you are *perceived* to be has an effect on what you have to say when you preach. Who you *are* is not the issue, but who your hearers *perceive* you to be. We may not like the sound of that,

but it is radically true. If people perceive you as a compassionate, caring person, they hear your words of compassion and care with their heads and hearts. But if your congregation considers you aloof and unapproachable, they will have trouble hearing and experiencing your message of compassion. Even if *you* feel you are warm and caring, the congregation's perceptions may be quite different.

Following a sermon in a preaching lab, students were giving their peer evaluation. One of them asked, "Why were you mad as you were preaching?"

A surprised, puzzled look crossed the student-preacher's face, and he retorted, "I wasn't mad."

But another student chimed in politely, "I sensed it too; it made me a bit uneasy."

Then the class reviewed the sermon on videotape. The preacher often frowned as he emphasized an idea; his voice also got louder and deeper at those points. Some students perceived the frowning and deepened voice as expressing anger.

The student-preacher was not angry, but his peers *perceived* that he was angry; that perception affected how they heard his sermon. He spent some time practicing in front of a mirror and successfully eliminated both his frowning and the negative critique of his preaching.

A congregation's expectations of its minister often affect its perceptions of the minister. Too often a congregation's expectations are totally unrealistic. As a child, I couldn't wait for the television announcer on my favorite show to say, "Faster than a speeding bullet; more powerful than a locomotive; able to leap tall buildings in a single bound." Little did I know then that the description of Superman would fit the criteria used by pastor-selection committees in their search process.

If the church's previous pastor had a "superminister" complex, you can imagine how they expect you to be: never tiring, able to work eighty or ninety hours a week without a break, always fresh as a daisy, never cranky, takes time to be with family and friends, never too tired for a late-night committee meeting and a six-o'clock breakfast the next morning with the elders of the church. How will they perceive you and your ministry when you fail to measure up to those expectations? The tragedy is that many pastors spend their entire ministries trying to live up to the unrealistic expectations and perceptions of congregations.

Since perceptions are so powerfully controlling, we want our hearers to perceive us as we really are. Some questions naturally arise: How do they perceive me? Who do they think I am? These questions fall within the realm of next chapter's discussion on congregation analysis. For now, the questions turn our attention to identification. We want to identify with our hearers, and we want them to identify with us.

What characteristics should you demonstrate to help the congregation perceive the real you and, in so doing, identify with you? The following traits are some nonnegotiables in minister-congregation relationships. This list is not exhaustive, and the order in which I present them does not constitute any form of priority. My desire is that these will stir your imagination. You will want to expand the list of nonnegotiables for your immediate pastoral setting, and help your hearers perceive you as you really are.

A Person of Integrity

A minister should be a person of integrity. At first glance, that statement appears so obvious that it borders on the ridiculous. There was a time when people automatically assumed ministers to be above reproach. People often placed the pastor of a local church on a pedestal as the model Christian for the community. Community leaders considered pastors to be moral beacons, faithfully shining across the shifting sea of societal values.

But within the past five to ten years, the moral failures of key religious and political figures, those who held communal trust, have been exposed. The result has been uneasiness and cynicism—a new unwillingness to trust the integrity of such leaders. Accounts of plagiarized papers and extramarital affairs tainted political campaigns in the 1980s and became the downfall of two presidential candidates. Moral indiscretion embarrassed the family and harmed the reputation of one national religious figure; financial impropriety caused another to face a stiff prison sentence. The role security that once came with the title "preacher" or "pastor" is no longer there. Ministers must work at ensuring and communicating their integrity.

A preacher demonstrates integrity when the sermon squares with his or her life. In other words, we must practice what we preach. Preaching is the most visible form of ministry that we do. Whether we like it or not, we place our total ministry under the microscope when we preach. Our congregations measure what we say in our sermons in the light of our lives and ministries beyond the pulpit.

Picture a minister who does not particularly like hospital visitation. His typical approach is something like this: Entering a hospital room, he nervously stands at the patient's bedside. The patient offers him a chair, but he declines. His remarks are stilted, almost as if he had memorized lines: "Well, how are you doing? How's the food? When will they let you come home? Well, I don't want to tire you out. How about if we pray?" The entire encounter lasts no more than four minutes.

Now, how will the parishioner feel when he or she returns to church and hears this pastor preaching, "Beloved, if you want to be like Christ you are going to have to take time to be with people. I mean really get to know them, hear their hurts and sorrows. That's what it means to be a Christian." If you were a patient he'd visited, would he convince you? What would you think? How would you react?

Then there are ministers who hold up their families as Christian models when everyone knows their kids are the terror of the neighborhood. Remember, the parishioners see you when you lose your patience with your child in the parking lot; they hear you when you voice anger to your spouse during a church potluck. They will forgive you for these transgressions. But they will not be forgiving of the breach of integrity when you make yourself out to be a model parent in your sermons.

Preaching that identifies and maintains integrity speaks of the realities and frustrations of family life in our fast-paced society. Help your congregation experience the grace and forgiveness of God by sharing how that grace has enabled you to cope with the difficulties of parenting. Confessional preaching creates identification. Imagine how your listeners will sit up in the pews and pay attention when you say, "I have a hard time being a patient parent." They identify with that struggle against impatience; as one of them, you help them hear the grace of the gospel.

Keep Your Promises

Another aspect of integrity is doing what you say you are going to do. Perhaps the most common ministerial remark is "Well, I'll be praying for you." Do we really mean that when we say it? Or is it simply the "ministerial" way of ending a conversation or counseling session?

If we say we're going to pray for someone, I hope that we honor that promise by praying. Will your parishioner ever know if you prayed? I wonder. We must be careful of the little promises we make. Those remarks that we take lightly might be taken seriously by a church member.

If you say at the close of a pastoral visit, "I'll give you a call next week to see how you're doing," you'd better make sure you do call. If you tell patients in the hospital that you'll be back in a day or two to see how they are progressing, make good on that promise. The damage to your integrity if you do not can be immeasurable. Passing remarks that we might forget seconds after making them are considered broken promises if we fail to make good. It's better to avoid saying you'll do things but then later to do them than to say that you will do them and forget. And every word you utter from the pulpit is measured against the congregation's perception of you.

A hidden question in the back of people's minds is, Can you be trusted? If information shared in counseling sessions becomes an illustration in Sunday's sermon, you failed the trustworthiness test; your integrity is called into question. Your hearers will not share the pains of their hearts with you for fear of becoming the showpiece for one of your sermons. Once broken, trust takes a long time to mend. If your trustworthiness is called into question, your pulpit effectiveness will be diminished and perhaps even lost.

Integrity in Preparation
Integrity also has to do with the type of sermon preparation that we do. There is a difference between authentic biblical and theological study and merely working to "get up a sermon." The former springs from an intense interest in finding truth and discovering contemporary ways to communicate that truth; the latter is "sermonizing" without interest in discovering or communicating the truths of the Bible in a relevant way. In this mode, preaching is a painful obligation: "I have to preach a sermon. Let me get this over with." Or, "I know what these people need to hear; let me work up a sermon so they can hear it."

Studying with integrity means that when we discover that a text contradicts our preconceived theological notions, we are willing to change our minds in light of biblical truth. The greatest obstacle Jesus faced with the Pharisees was not a lack of scriptural knowledge, but their unwillingness to change their minds when he confronted them with new understandings about Scripture: "The sabbath was made for humankind, and not humankind for the sabbath" (Mk 2:27). Preparation with integrity means that one approaches sermon study with an open mind and a desire to experience something new, rather than merely going to the Bible to find support for one's preformed convictions.

Integrity in preparation also has to do with how we use other people's material. Using another's material without giving credit or acknowledging that the ideas are not one's own raises questions of integrity. Since sermon preparation is a process of synthesizing much of what we read and hear, when should you give credit? A rule of thumb is that if you are asking yourself, "Should I give credit for this idea?" it's best to err on the side of grace and give credit. If you do not, some in your congregation may be familiar with the material you are using and they'll realize that you are stealing ideas. Also, if you do not give credit for another's ideas, your congregation might wonder why you are so insightful in your sermons yet not so in church council meetings.

How much do you have to say in giving credit? Saying something as simple as "I read . . ." or "I heard . . ." lets the congregation know that the idea or story is not yours. You show that it is someone else's, that it has enriched you and you want to share it with them. Your hearers will appreciate your efforts in preparation and your honesty.

This idea holds true for sermon illustrations. Never tell someone else's incident or story as though it happened to you. The only word for that is dishonesty. You can tell another person's story with just as much effect and conviction when you tell it about him or her.

Tony Campolo tells a story of throwing a birthday party for a prostitute at half past three in the morning at a greasy-spoon restaurant in Honolulu.[2] It's a wonderful story of grace, and a challenge to the church to do what only the church can do.

Now, it would be audacious for you or me to tell that story as though it happened to us. But we can tell the story: "Tony Campolo was in Honolulu, Hawaii, and had an unbelievable experience . . ."

My suggestion is not that you spend a lot of sermon time footnoting sources for your hearers. Laypeople sometimes complain that preachers drop too many names to impress the congregation with whom or how much they know. (What do you think that does to the integrity scoreboard?) If knowing the name of the quoted person or theologian is germane to the point you're making, then use the name; if not, avoid it. "A theologian said" may do more for the point you are making than "Karl Barth, perhaps the most profound theologian of this century, said . . ." Consider your hearers, consider what you are quoting and then make the best decision based on the purpose of the sermon.

The tactics some preachers use to provoke a desired response may indicate inadequate preparation. Suppose a preacher has not spent enough preparation time and realizes that the sermon is deficient. To compensate for the inadequate preparation, the preacher ends the sermon with a "dying dog" story. The story of the little child holding her dying dog brings tears to the eyes and folks into the aisles.

That tactic is manipulative and dishonest. There is a place for authentic emotions in preaching, but not as a cover for inadequate preparation.

Other Concerns

Your active participation in worship communicates that you have integrity. Some ministers pay almost no attention to what is going on during the worship service. They thumb through their Bibles while the choir is singing. During the special music, they underline an important sentence in their outline. This communicates to the congregation that what happens before the preacher steps up to the pulpit is only preliminaries, not really important. The congregation watches us as we participate in worship. They watch us as we sing the hymns of the faith; they even watch us while others are praying. Integrity is perceived as we connect with them, faithful participants in the worship of God, just as they are.

Of course, any discussion of integrity should deal with general issues of good and ethical conduct for ministers, such as financial and sexual morality. The minister's ethical conduct in all aspects of life has a direct impact on his or her preaching ministry. Books on ministerial ethics cover these topics in depth. Do not misunderstand my brevity here as minimizing the importance of integrity in these areas. The temptations we've looked at in this section are more subtle and therefore more widespread.

What you say in your sermons, how you use illustrations, how you share your humanity, how you put your life into your preaching—through your actions outside the pulpit and through what you say when you preach—demonstrate the kind of person you are. If your congregation perceives that you are a person of integrity, you are well on the way to creating identification with your hearers.

An Authentic Person
The character of a minister is often stated in terms of authenticity. Does your congregation perceive you to be a *real* person? Or do they perceive that you are unreal, a plastic figure without struggles or feelings? Through our preaching we can communicate that we have a deep sense of sin and forgiveness; we understand grace because we are recipients of it.

A minister once challenged me on this point. He argued that his congregation did not want to see weakness in the pulpit; they did not want to hear that he struggled with doubt or sin. They expected him to give them the answers to their struggles.

I wonder how that church understands Paul's statement "All have sinned and fall short of the glory of God" (Rom 3:23). My opinion is that their theology of preaching has reformulated the verse to sound like this: "*Except for our pastor,* all have sinned . . ." We should confess our struggles, and most people will see and appreciate our honesty.

Recognize Your Humanity

Authenticity has to do with recognizing one's humanity. In my early years of ministry, I had the "unhuman" notion that ministers were omniscient, all-knowing, when it came to matters of the church and theology. I thought people expected me to have all the answers to questions ranging from the challenge of neo-orthodoxy to how a church member should deal with grief over the death of a spouse.

An insightful mentor asked me why I had a "God-complex." He said, "You act like the ministerial version of the Shell answer man." The Shell Oil Company's "answer man" had an answer to every problem one could think of about an automobile: questions about brakes, mufflers, fuel injection systems, windshield wipers. He had all the answers—no ambiguity, just answers. I was attempting to do the same thing when it came to the things of God.

When we recognize our humanity, we help those to whom we minister come to grips with theirs. Church members often question their Christianity when they find themselves struggling with doubt, yet their minister may seem to have all answers and no questions. Raymond Bailey's definition of faith is helpful here. He says faith is "giving as much of yourself as you understand to as much of God as you understand at that moment." Understanding and recognizing our humanity is a crucial element for faith.

Recognizing one's humanity is also a way of recognizing God's divinity. I think this is what Paul meant when he said,

"But he said to me, 'My grace is sufficient for you, for [my] power is made perfect in weakness.' So, I will boast all the more gladly of my weaknesses, so that the power of Christ may dwell in me. . . . for whenever I am weak, then I am strong" (2 Cor 12:9-10). In his recognition of his humanity, Paul truly experienced God's grace..

Another sign of authenticity is a healthy sense of humor. One of my teachers admonished me to take the gospel seriously but never to take myself too seriously. When words like "stress" and "burnout" describe the state of many in ministry, the ability to laugh at oneself and enjoy life is a needed antidote. Ministers must learn to lighten up a bit. We can learn much from the contemporary teenage admonition to "chill out"—translated "calm down, relax, laugh a little." I wonder if that is what gospel, good news, might really mean.

A sense of humor communicates a feeling of joy about life. The church, the one community where joy should overflow, is often afraid to express real joy. Have you ever heard a congregation sing the wonderful children's chorus about joy: "I've got that joy, joy, joy, joy down in my heart"? Usually they sing it like a funeral dirge. I don't know what they have in their hearts, but it's not joy! (Maybe Maalox will take care of it.) Just a little joy, a sense of humor, makes it possible to laugh at oneself and to enjoy life.

Another facet of communicating authenticity has to do with understanding one's limits. Know your limitations. Perhaps the operative word here is *humility*. Do not pretend to be more than you are. We do not realize how transparent we are to our parishioners when it comes to our own limitations. They can usually tell when we're operating beyond our limits. For example, most ministers have had some formal training in counseling, usually within their seminary education. That training is usually general in nature. When it comes to counseling, know your limitations. Don't play psychiatrist from the pulpit unless you are one.

Perhaps it goes back to congregational expectations, but many ministers think they have to know everything and be an expert about everything. What did you think about know-it-alls when you were a kid? I hated them too! My definition of a know-it-all is a person who knows nothing about everything. As a preacher, know your limits. Authentic ministers can say, "I don't know." Your congregation will perceive and appreciate that, and they will hear you when you preach.

On the other hand, don't pretend to be less than you are. I have heard seminary graduates try to create identification by denigrating their education: "I might have a Ph.D., but that doesn't keep me from being just like you." What does that really say? Congregations perceive pretending to be less than you are as condescension, which is no asset when you are attempting to communicate with them.

A question you might ask yourself is, How comfortable am I with whom I am? When you are comfortable with yourself, you do not have to be more or less; you can just be yourself. I played drums in a rock-and-roll band while in high school in the sixties. Our band's bass player looked like Adonis incarnate. He had muscles and beautiful long blond hair, and he always said the right thing. I was chubby, wore glasses and had short black hair—and it seemed I *never* said the right thing. When Bill walked into a room, the girls would swoon; when I walked into a room, the girls would leave!

Needless to say, I was not comfortable with myself. I thought if I could look like Bill then I would be like him. So I talked my mother into buying me an outfit just like he wore: white bell-bottom pants, a white turtleneck sweater, a navy blue pea coat with black anchor buttons, and Beatle boots like Lennon's and McCartney's. I never admitted it then, but when I put on that outfit, I still didn't look like Bill; and wearing it did not make me any more popular with anyone. In fact, I looked ridiculous because it "wasn't me."

Today I often see Christians and ministers trying to do the same thing. People who aren't comfortable with who they are, trying to be somebody else. Trying to preach like a television personality, attempting to be the "big-city" pastor, is not authentic. Our congregations see right through the façade and have trouble taking us seriously when we preach.

Maintain Healthy Relationships

Healthy relationships are mandatory for identification, and openness is one necessary ingredient for relationships. Many pastors find it difficult to be open with their congregations for fear that they would appear weak and vulnerable if people really knew them. This obviously gets back to our earlier discussion about expectations. I know that some churches treat openness as a weakness; yet even those congregations can be led to understand that openness is a hallmark of the gospel. I think many ministers hide behind the myths of expectations created by previous generations, with no desire to change the status quo. Studies show that congregations long for openness in their ministers.[3] Your openness promotes relationship, and relationship is crucial for identification.

Another way to develop relationships is by being approachable. I have heard people say, "Oh, I could never talk to my pastor about that; anyhow, he's too busy." I wonder if they were really saying that their pastor was not approachable. Approachability, again, is something that the congregation experiences by perception. No one wears a sign that says, "Talk to me, I'm approachable" or "Unapproachable—stay clear." Or do we? Judgmental comments about people, a lackadaisical attitude toward church work, standoffishness and flaunting one's education all communicate that one is unapproachable.

I knew a minister with an earned doctorate who demanded that church members use the title "Dr." in addressing him. How approachable do you think that congregation perceived the minister to be when they could never talk to him on a first-name basis?

Accessibility goes hand in hand with approachability. You might be perceived as approachable but never accessible. Some pastors never have time for anyone. They seem always on the run.

You've met people like that. You stop them in a hallway to talk for a second, or you speak to them in their office, and it's obvious that they just don't have time for you. Their minds are a million miles away; the lights are on, but nobody is home. They're friendly enough, but they're always preoccupied. How would you hear a sermon from a person who never had time to listen to you?

Congregations identify with authentic ministers. As you recognize your humanity, you give your hearers permission to recognize theirs. As you are open and approachable, you communicate values essential for healthy relationships. Being an authentic person is vital for creating identification with any group of hearers.

A Person of Faith

There's nothing sadder than to see ministers whose souls are parched and withered from giving so much without taking time to replenish themselves spiritually. The irony of ministry is that the demands—hospital visitation, prospect visitation, counseling, preaching, administration, continuing education—are so great that busy ministers may actually neglect their own spiritual nurture. Surrounded by the things of God, pastors often confuse doing ministry with developing their lives of faith. While doing ministry is a part of faith development, it is not the only part.

Congregations expect their pastors to be people of faith. In my opinion, this is a nonnegotiable characteristic of ministerial personhood. We all have heard sermons in which the preacher encouraged us to spend more time in prayer, more time in personal Bible study, more time developing our devotional lives. I hope those preachers practiced what they preached.

Our best preaching, preaching that identifies with the lives of our hearers, preaching that creates identification between ourselves and God, emerges out of a genuine growing faith. Faith is the substance of our lives for ministry. Kenneth Burke says that the word *substance* contains a paradox.[4] It means that which stands under something—that is, sub stance. Substance also refers to the essence of a thing, the material of which something is made. Faith undergirds us when we preach; faith is the support upon which our preaching stands. It is the foundation from which we live and move and have our being. But faith is also the essence, the substance, of our preaching. We do not preach politics or science or humanistic philosophy; we preach the gospel "revealed through faith for faith" (Rom 1:17). Faith is the substance of our preaching; therefore, preachers must be people of authentic faith.

We encounter God in a growing faith relationship. That encounter drives us to the pulpit to proclaim good news. Our preaching is not just a report on events that took place two thousand years ago, but a testimony to our continuing encounter with the Lord of the gospel. Because we have met God, we desperately want others to identify themselves with the salvation offered in Christ. I like the way John puts it:

We declare to you what was from the beginning, what we have heard, what we have seen with our eyes, what we have looked at and touched with our hands, concerning the word of life. . . . we declare to you what we have seen and heard so that you also may have fellowship with us; and truly our fellowship is with the Father and with his Son Jesus Christ. (1 Jn 1:1-3)

Our faith relationship with God is what empowers our preaching. Our congregations expect us to be people of faith.

Physical well-being is part of a holistic pilgrimage of faith. Ministers often neglect the physical side of spiritual well-being. Taking time for exercise, watching what one eats and making time for leisure activities do not sound like especially spiritual activities. But remember, the Docetic heresy was that Jesus only appeared to be human. His body was a mirage; he was only a spirit, went the teaching. Ministers drift toward a sort of practical heresy today when they forget that their spirituality contains a physical dimension.

When doing seminars on the subject, I always hear the argument that there is not enough time in the day to get everything done as it is, without taking time to exercise. Another argument is that ministers are on the go; they don't have time to eat right, so they have no choice but to gobble down cholesterol-laden fast food. It amazes me to hear such arguments from people who preach every Sunday to encourage their hearers to change their behavior.

Being a person of faith means attempting to model characteristics of healthy living that glorify the God who created us as physical and spiritual beings. A little-exercised body that has trouble walking up stairs brings no glory to God. It takes only an hour three or four times a week to provide a healthy amount of exercise for the average person. Ministers who exercise attest that they have more energy, are more alert and can accomplish more in less time than they did before their exercise program.

I know this is sounding like a TV commercial for a weight-loss beverage, but a holistic theology of body, mind and spirit is essential for the person of faith.

Effective ministry is difficult. We sometimes assume that a person of faith never has faith struggles. But the opposite is true. We've all been ready to throw in the towel now and again. When days are tough and your ministry seems like a futile task, remember whose you are and remember your call to ministry. A friend told me there will be days when your sense of call is all you have to keep going. Relying on faith may be the best way to demonstrate that you are a person of faith.

A Competent Minister

People expect preachers to be competent ministers of the gospel. When a person goes to a medical doctor, he expects that the doctor is a competent practitioner, that she spends time honing her medical skills, that she is working to be the best doctor she can be. Why should people expect anything less from ministers of the gospel?

Paul's admonition to the Ephesians reminds us "to walk worthy of the calling to which we have been called" (Eph 4:1). People who listen to our sermons expect that our preaching will reflect our training as practical theologians. People should rightly expect us to be competent in biblical interpretation and theological reflection. That is the area in which we have been trained and to which we have dedicated our lives.

To remain competent, preachers must be committed to a lifetime of learning and study. Many ministers find making time for study difficult because they do not view study time as ministry. They understand ministry in narrow terms of direct face-to-face encounters with people; and study time keeps them from being with people. But understood in the broadest sense, ministry includes all that we do pastorally in the care of our congregations. Study time enhances both our preaching ministry and one-on-one counseling and encouragement.

We must also understand that a variety of ministries can be accomplished from the pulpit. Pastoral care, teaching, encouraging and evangelism are but a few of the ways that direct ministry is accomplished from the pulpit. To gain the kinds of competencies necessary to offer these ministries, preachers must be dedicated and disciplined students of the Bible, of theology, of life.

We demonstrate our competence as ministers in our performance. Ministry is hard work, and effective ministers are not afraid of hard work. Being with people, caring for people and juggling study time and family time create tremendous demands on us. Learning to ask the right questions, spending time finding out what the questions are and not giving answers where there are none are ways that we demonstrate our competence to the members of our churches.

An overlooked issue of competence is that preachers must earn the right to be heard. Many ministers assume that their call to a pastorate guarantees that they will be heard when they preach. Such an attitude has been the downfall of many preachers; they confused *role* authority with *real* authority. Managerial training in the business world and leadership training in the military reminds those in charge that, though they have the rank of leadership, they are not leaders of the people until the people make them the leaders. An authoritarian officer can get the job done; a *real* leader has the potential to move the people beyond the minimum.

Competent ministers are authorities in the field of ministry. They lead out of a commitment to the congregation that called them, out of a commitment to the call of God on their lives. Congregations expect their ministers to exercise appropriate authority.

Do not confuse *authoritative* with *authoritarian* or *autocratic*. Remember, Jesus astounded the people because he taught them "as one having authority" (Mt 7:29). Parishioners give you authority when the congregation calls you; they expand that authority as you minister to them, demonstrate your competence among them, become one with them.

When people go to the doctor, they expect to be treated by a competent physician who knows what he or she is doing. That expectation should be no less for ministers. Effective ministers create identification with their congregations through their competence.

Concern for People

A pastor insightfully stated: "People don't care how much you know until they know how much you care."[5] The core of identification in preaching is to let the people know you sincerely care about them. In one way or another your hearers will ask, Do you really care about us? They will watch when we ask, "How's your family doing?" to see whether we really care about their family or are just being polite. A ninety-year-old woman, speaking to her pastor, said it this way: "You have learned what the human touch really means. You love us."[6]

Charles Laughton, known for his prowess as an actor, also loved to do interpretive reading. The following quotation is attributed to him: "Good reading is reading something you love to someone you love." A colleague modified the idea for preaching: "Good preaching is preaching something you love to those you love." Is that not a wonderful picture?

How do we show an entire congregation that we love them? Words such as *compassion, empathy, sympathy,* as well as their negative counterpart *apathy,* come to mind. The root for these words is the Greek word *pathos,* from which we derive the English word *passion.* Preachers who identify with their congregations communicate a passion about what they preach, a passion for people, a passion for the gospel, a passion for life.

From the Pulpit

How does one demonstrate a sincere concern, a passion, for people from the pulpit? Enthusiasm is key. We think of this word as meaning eagerness or excitement. But the Greek root of the word, *en theos,* means inspired of God—a phrase that should apply to our preaching, I think. Preaching should demonstrate eagerness and enthusiasm. Lethargy from the pulpit breeds lethargy. Perhaps the downfall of preaching in the late twentieth century has been the proliferation of *passionless* preaching.

Enthusiasm from the pulpit does not meaning running back and forth on the platform hooting and hollering. It has to do, again, with the image you project. Enthusiasm imbues the subject with a sense of importance. It also projects concern for your hearers; they will more readily identify with you if they sense your excitement about what is taking place. Your tone of voice, the way the sermon physically engages you, the degree to which you believe in what you are preaching and the extent to which you explicitly show a concern for your hearers communicate enthusiasm.

The kind of language you use also demonstrates your concern for people. Probably the most sensitive issue today is the use of inclusive language. Masculinized language dominated the pulpits of America until the early 1980s. Many older ministers continue to refer to all people as "men" without a second thought. Even when confronted, they say they are being inclusive, for *men* refers to men and women. Unfortunately, in today's context that argument no longer holds water.

The legal and medical professions and the business world use inclusive language. Why is it that preachers are so reluctant to follow suit? My impression is that many ministers view inclusive language as an obsession of "radical feminists." In an attempt to be "not of the world," preachers stick to exclusive language, thereby maintaining "orthodoxy."

Our reason for using inclusive language should not be to copy what others are doing. Our impetus is that the gospel requires inclusion. If we learn anything about the kingdom of God from Jesus, it is that the kingdom is available to all people. Our language should model that. In preaching, we want to identify explicitly with all our hearers: men, women, children, senior adults, youth, single people, married people and people with disabilities should know that our message includes them.

Inclusive language is sometimes awkward in speech. It means that we have to say "he and she," or we have to turn singulars into plurals. It takes work to break the habit of exclusive language, but the gospel message is worth it. Could it be said that the gospel demands it? People will identify with us and the good news we preach when they are sure, without any doubt, that we include them.

Another language issue has to do with the use of theological jargon. Why is it that we get angry when doctors use medical terms to describe our condition, yet we will go right to the pulpit and lay theological terms on our hearers? Most of your hearers haven't the foggiest idea what "the eschatological implications of the parousia" means. Show your hearers you care for them by using language they understand, language that is part of their everyday experience, language to which they can identify.

It's not always easy to purge one's vocabulary of technical language. One way is to tape your sermons and listen to them with someone who will honestly critique the words you used. I find that teenagers in the congregation are more than happy to oblige. You will be amazed at how many theological terms slip in without your awareness. Purging your sermons of these terms and translating them into the language of your people is an intentional way to create identification.

Finally, never embarrass your family or close acquaintances from the pulpit. Now that you have read that rule, you are probably thinking that preachers should never embarrass *anyone* from the pulpit. You are absolutely right. The reason I emphasize close friends, and especially family, is that we might assume that embarrassing them is all right because we are close to them. Not so. No one likes being embarrassed. Be careful about using stories having to do with family and friends. Show your concern for others by showing concern for the people closest to you. Your hearers can identify with that.

In Daily Life
How does one demonstrate a passion for people outside the

pulpit? Identification in preaching is not only measured by what you do in the pulpit; your "nonpreaching" behavior also helps create or prevent identification.   People watch to see how you respond to crisis in their lives and in the lives of other church members. Being there in times of need is crucial for establishing identification. Also, simple remembrances of special events such as anniversaries and birthdays are an excellent way to build ongoing rapport with your congregation. While in the pastorate, I signed a birthday card for each church member and included personal words of congratulation. This took some time each week; but it was more than worth it in terms of creating identification.

One pastor put it this way: Pastors must establish "a reserve of grace" with their congregations.[7] That is what I'm suggesting. In or out of the pulpit, when you let people know that you care for them, you build more than a reserve of grace; you will truly connect with them.

Summing Up

Who you are perceived to be has an effect on your preaching message and how it is heard. In this chapter we've considered important characteristics you must demonstrate if you are to create authentic identification with your congregation. In the next chapter we turn attention away from you and toward the congregation. Who are my hearers? How can I understand them better? How do I learn what my congregation is all about? This is the next step in becoming one with them.

5/Taking Stock
of Your Scene

Communication cannot be satisfactory unless the matter discussed
bears in some notable respect upon the interests of the auditor.
KENNETH BURKE, *PERMANENCE AND CHANGE*

*I*n a study of quality in pastoral ministry, a section called "Prelude to Failure" addresses the question "Where do ministers set
themselves up for failure?" A panel discussion produced possible answers: "they don't know their people"; "they don't know
the expectations of their people"; "they fight traditions"; "they
initiate change too rapidly"; "they don't discern who the decision makers are." John Dever interpreted the remarks by saying
that "the pastor is doomed to failure if he or she does not take
time to get to know the church, the people, and the community."[1] These issues stand at the heart of identification.

Preaching never takes place in a vacuum. We saw in chapter
three how biblical characters modeled effective preaching because they were sensitive to their contexts; they identified with
their hearers. They understood their hearers' theological, philosophical, ideological, sociological, economic, political and
physical contexts. In other words, they knew their people. Kenneth Burke would say that they understood their preaching
scene because communication is always "*circumstantially*
founded."[2] "The rich man's prayer is not the poor man's

prayer," says Burke.[3] What makes the prayers different is their circumstances, scenes, contexts.

The identification process begins when the preacher analyzes the congregational scene. Getting to know your hearers and identifying with them begins with a knowledge of the contexts that affect them. We must be intentional about considering the various contexts in which our hearers live. These contexts are the container in which we preach and minister.[4] Just as a fluid is influenced by the shape of its container, the life of our congregation is influenced and shaped by the contextual container of the world in which the parishioners live and move and have their being. The world around you is the context for your preaching; the first step in congregational analysis is intentionally to take stock of that world.

I must sound a warning here. Our zeal to identify quickly with our hearers can actually create the opposite effect. We run the risk of giving primary attention to the most immediate influences on a particular congregation. If you serve a rural church made up primarily of farmers, you'll make a mistake if you begin your congregational analysis by surveying the immediate problems and concerns farmers face. If your congregation is made up of professional people in a growing community in the suburbs, be careful that you do not begin your congregational analysis by assuming that the latest report on the lifestyle of baby boomers and baby busters applies to your parishioners.

Burke suggests that an ever-expanding series of factors, like the circles that unfurl when you drop a pebble into water, surround and influence every immediate scene. Every outside ring has an effect on the next adjacent ring. To understand situations adequately, we should look beyond the immediate context to the factors that make up the expanded contextual scene. For example, when we apply this idea to a discussion about family, we could talk in terms of immediate family—mother, father, sister, brother—then broaden our discussion to extended family—aunts, uncles, cousins, nieces, nephews—and expand it even more to the family of humankind. Burke calls this the concern for the scene's "circumference."[5]

If we are to understand our congregations adequately, and if our preaching is going to address their needs, then we must evaluate the congregation in terms of their scene and the circumferences that make it up. Burke believes that when we appropriately understand the scene, we can develop effective rhetorical responses to it; for preaching, these responses are shaped into sermons.

We will begin our discussion with the farthest circumference, the world scene. Then we will narrow the examination to the cultural scene, the religious scene, and finally the congregational scene—the context that most directly affects your hearers. You will get to know your hearers and identify with them by knowing their contexts.

The World Scene

The modern world is a small world. With the proliferation of fiber-optic transmission through beams of light, microwave links and satellites, information is available to us instantaneously. News stories that once took days or hours for networks to telecast are now beamed instantly into our living rooms. Once we were happy to have the evening news bring us up to date on the day's events. Now we watch many events as they happen.

I was in the Air Force in the early seventies, during the Vietnam War. Each night my wife and I watched the news with increasing concern, because I was on active duty. The broadcaster provided battle statistics of recent days and showed newsreel footage of helicopters on the move and soldiers digging in for the next fray.

How things have changed today! In the summer of 1990, Iraq invaded Kuwait; we heard about it within hours. In January

1991, the United States led a coalition of forces to liberate Kuwait. We watched and listened as CNN broadcast from within a hotel in the heart of Baghdad. Bernard Shaw and John Holliman, CNN correspondents, described the "surgical accuracy" of Tomahawk missiles. We watched videotaped replays of laser-guided "smart bombs" dropping into air vents in selected targets. Our anxiety heightened as sirens wailed in Tel Aviv, warning inhabitants of the imminent arrival of Iraqi Scud missiles. Daily, millions of Americans glued themselves to television sets and heard briefings from central command in Riyadh, Saudi Arabia. General Norman Schwarzkopf talked to the world about the progress of the war. The Pentagon received much information at the same time we did. We watched news happen.

New Political Realities
Another factor affecting the world scene is the rapidly changing political climate. In 1980, who would have predicted the collapse of the Berlin Wall, the passionate call for democracy in Eastern Bloc countries, the disintegration of communism and the dissolution of the Soviet Union? Some of you remember the Cold War and the paranoia we lived under in the early sixties. I was a young teenager and remember air raid drills at school. Many families in our neighborhood had some sort of bomb shelter in their homes; the Civil Defense produced television commercials that described the provisions every home should lay up in case there was a nuclear attack from "the Russians." That is how my grandfather Fowler referred to them—"the Russians." McCarthyism had convinced him and many other Americans that there was a communist under every rock and behind every tree. The world scene is much different today.

The political climate in the world today is one of guarded optimism. Hope for peace in the Middle East is real, though it is fragile. The democratic spirit that spread across the world in the closing decade of the eighties continues unabated in the nineties. No one is foolish enough to attempt to predict the future, but the current world scene is not as threatening as it was even five years ago.

More people than ever before are developing a global view. For instance, concern for the environment is not an American issue, or a British issue, or a European issue, or a Japanese issue; it is a world issue. Children learn about the environment in school. They learn about the delicate balance of nature. They understand that fluorocarbons contained in aerosol spray cans deplete the ozone layer. Our children are growing up with a knowledge that natural resources will not last forever. The world in which we live is the only world we have; we must take care of it. Children learn about recycling, and they teach their families how to shop for environmentally friendly products. Americans who once engaged in rampant consumerism are taking stock of their behavior because of environmental threats. We realize that what we do affects others.

Changing Economic Realities

A new world order has produced interesting economic phenomena. The interdependence of trade among nations makes isolationism, once thought a viable economic policy, virtually impossible. Listen to the daily business reports on the radio. The Tokyo stock exchange affects the London stock exchange, which affects the New York stock exchange, which in turn affects the Tokyo exchange the next day. We hear daily about the balance of trade and trade deficits. American companies plead with us to "buy American," but at the same time many Americans are working in the United States for foreign-owned companies. Buying American provides jobs for some Americans, but in the current economic climate, it will likely put others in the unemployment line.

The World and the Pulpit

What does all of this have to do with preaching? Is analyzing the world scene really necessary? A student said to me during a class discussion, "The church where I pastor is a small country church. My members don't care about global issues. They don't understand a thing about international economics. They're worried about their families and their farms and how they're going to pay the rent."

This discussion took place during Operation Desert Storm's liberation of Kuwait. I asked him whether any of his church members were involved in the conflict. He said that one was in an army unit near the front lines and that a member's nephew was a navy pilot on an aircraft carrier. Then I asked, "Doesn't what happens in Iraq affect your church family?" He nodded in contemplative agreement.

I could have carried the debate into other areas, such as grain prices. The price his parishioners pay for grain to feed their cattle is not fixed locally. The international economy influences the price of grain—even locally produced grain.

His response to me was interesting: "Well, things that happen in the world may affect my hearers, but I still don't think they look at it that way." He may be right. Though his hearers may not be interested in what goes on in the world, they are still affected by it. As preachers, we must be aware of the influences, whether local or international, that affect our hearers.

Hear me carefully at this point. I am not suggesting that you evaluate the world scene so you can preach about it. If you turn every newspaper headline into the topic for next Sunday's sermon, you will wear thin your welcome with your congregation. Sure, you'll find a sermon illustration in the story of the collapsing Berlin Wall. But our analysis of the world scene transcends the search for illustrative material. The point of studying the world scene is that it's one of the contexts affecting your hearers. If you are going to identify with them and preach to their needs, you must be aware of their entire world.

The Cultural Scene

Moving from the world scene to the next smaller circumference, we find ourselves in the midst of the cultural scene. There are many approaches we could take in looking at this context. Perhaps the most obvious to consider is that we live in a technologically sophisticated society. New technology affects the cars we drive (computer-controlled fuel injection systems and antilock brakes), how we entertain ourselves (VCRs show movies-to-go in our living rooms; laser compact discs provide distortion-free music), how we control the environment in our homes (servo-controlled feedback systems) and how we educate our children (computer programs to aid and supplement classroom learning). The most notable characteristic of a technology-based society, however, is its reliance on sending, receiving and handling information.

Earlier this century, a large portion of the American population was agrarian. People earned money through the production of food crops and animal husbandry. Another major segment worked in industry, producing steel, automobiles, appliances and other material goods. People knew how productive they were because they could see what they produced. Economists measured success in terms of tangible productivity. But a technologically sophisticated society measures success in ways that are seldom tangible. Information is not an easily perceived asset. And it's harder for workers to take pride in their work when their achievements are subjective and difficult to discern.

Also, the face of the work force is changing. George Barna has noted that in 1990 approximately six million households had a least one head of household using the home as a work base.[6] Technology makes this kind of work possible. With the

advent of computer modems, FAX machines and cellular tele-
phones, one's office can be virtually anyplace—that is, anyplace
that has a plug for a computer.

Computers are smaller, faster, and available to everyone.
Children learn how to use them as part of the regular curriculum in school. Many of us have a computer on our desk at
work and another at home. We use them for writing reports and
letters, for keeping track of our finances, even for helping us
file our sermons. Next time you walk through an airport, notice
how many people carry laptop computers as part of their trav-
eling mode. Computers make our jobs easier, quicker and more
accurate. With them we can handle vast amounts of information. Already we would find it hard to make do without them.

Preachers, notice a warning flag! When our people work and
when they go to school, information inundates them; they experience information overload. What they dread, if only sub-
consciously, is coming to church and being fed more information. Have you ever said, "People complain that they don't
know what's going on in church. Why don't they read the bulletin or listen to the announcements"? Is it possible that they
are overloaded? What they need least in the world is more
information.

This possibility says something to us about the content of our
sermons. Do our sermons merely give people more information
about God? Or do they invite the congregation to an experience with God? We will consider these questions in the next
chapter when we look at sermon strategies. For now, notice that
our cultural context has forced us to ask the questions in the
first place.

In my opinion, the greatest problem with widespread technology is depersonalization. Do you still walk up to a teller
inside the bank? For months I haven't talked to, or for that
matter seen, a human being when I do my banking. I drive up
to an ATM machine, insert my plastic card with its magical

magnetic strip and make my transactions. The machine is never in a bad mood, has never had an argument with a spouse and did not have to get the kids off to school before coming to work. The machine knows my name; it even tells me to have a nice day. (How does it know what a nice day is?) It gets the job done, but something is missing.

Again, it always seems to happen just when we sit to eat dinner. Has it ever happened to you? The phone rings; I answer it. On the other end is a computer-controlled voice telling me that I've won a trip to Hawaii. If I want to claim the trip, and I'm at a touch-tone phone, I should press 1 and, for a minimal processing fee, I will soon be enjoying the beaches of Waikiki. Other times the voice reminds me that my lawn needs servicing, or a movie company needs extras for a production being filmed in town.

To avoid the interruptions, I let my answering machine talk to computerized calls. It only makes sense to make the best of what we have to put up with! You get the point. Technology can be helpful, but even "user-friendly" computers lack personality.

In conferences, when I say that depersonalization is the result of technology, some people argue that it is the other way around. People want to be left alone, and so they create technology. Their argument goes: "Why do you think people don't know their neighbors today? Why isn't there a community spirit in communities today? People want to be left alone." Personally, I am more optimistic about humans than that. Maybe the single most important thing we can learn from Jesus about ministry is the importance of the personal touch. Even in a technologically sophisticated society, the personal touch will never be obsolete.

Pluralism

Pluralism is another characteristic of our cultural scene. Our society is filled with diverse ethnic, racial, religious and social groups. Each group actively participates in the development of the larger society. Pluralism's strength is that each group brings new strengths to the whole. We can learn much from those who are different from us. As we learn from their customs and worldviews, we gain new perspectives on life. Society becomes more than a sum of its parts.

But a pluralistic society has inherent weaknesses as well. The special characteristics and qualities brought to the society by a group are swallowed up and lost in the whole. The merging of various cultures may lead to confusion of moral issues. The process of mixing dilutes each group's values and moral concerns.

Pluralistic societies tend to de-emphasize moral positions. In an attempt to prevent one group's morality from infringing on the rights of another group, moral and ethical concerns become obscured. To deal with morality, pluralistic societies turn to religious communities as the prescribers of moral codes. This action protects public schools and other institutions from having to make or enforce any moral code. A pluralistic society calls the prescription of a code of ethics a *religious issue.*

Consumerism

Another dilemma of the cultural scene is consumerism. Many baby boomers, those born between 1945 and 1960, absorb themselves with what I call the "angst of materialism"—the insatiable desire to have what they want when they want it. They grew up during a period of economic prosperity, do not know what it means to go without something and will not take no for an answer. Baby boomers set the tone for our society when it comes to materialism.

We consume ourselves to death with gadgets and devices; accumulating more things is a way of life. Most of us own VCRs. Have you bought the contraption that rewinds VHS cassettes so your VCR does not wear out (as fast)? Just another thing some people have to have.

An unwritten rule in our culture is that personal worth is measured in terms of what one owns. Who you are is directly proportional to what you have. Kids will not wear a regular pair of sneakers to play basketball. If you are the parent of a teenager, you have probably heard the question: "Do you want my friends to think I'm a geek?" The norm today is for teenagers to wear $150 designer athletic shoes that flaunt the name of the basketball star-of-the-day. I wonder where kids learn that kind of behavior.

Many dream of owning name-brand clothes, a status car, a home in a plush neighborhood, and some work relentlessly to fulfill these dreams. Consumerism produces a society bent on things.

In the midst of such a mindset, Jesus' words to the rich young man are hard to hear (Mt 19:21). We have the awesome responsibility of preaching the message that people's worth lies not in what they own, but in God's love for them. That is very good news, but for a congregation living in a consumer culture, the news is difficult to comprehend.

Family Life

The nature of family life must be a consideration when analyzing the cultural scene. Many families today are two-worker families. The father and mother both have jobs, and both of their incomes are necessary to make ends meet. The median cost of a single-family home is approximately $100,000; when monthly mortgage payments can exceed $1,000, a family needs two salaries.

Financial concerns are generally the reason that both parents work. But often career choices are involved as well. Men and women today pursue careers for more than financial reasons. A sense of accomplishment and a desire to make a difference in society motivate women and men to aspire to careers in business, law, medicine, ministry, engineering and many other professions.

When considering modern families, ministers must be careful not to assume that "family" means a husband, wife, two children, a dog and a white picket fence. Single-parent families are a reality in every community. To work, rear children and have a social life is a great struggle for single parents.

The issue of single-parent families is a good example of the church's failure to correctly analyze the cultural scene. Some denominational publications on family life still totally disregard issues facing single-parent families. In fact, nothing in the material even hints that single-parent families exist. How tragic that a denomination's concern for maintaining traditional family values would allow it to neglect a reality and a possibility for ministry in our society and our churches.

Blended families are another reality in contemporary culture. The first blended family most of us became familiar with was the Brady Bunch, popular on television in the seventies. A woman with three daughters meets a man who has three sons; they marry, and the whole clan lives happily ever after. (Only on television.) Though the program modeled healthy family values, this his-hers-and-ours sitcom romanticized the multiple complex factors involved in making blended families work. If your church does not have several blended families already, you are probably the exception. Does your preaching ever address the needs faced by these special family units?

If we are going to speak adequately to people's needs through preaching, we have to know what those needs are. Analyzing the cultural scene is a crucial step in knowing how the society around us affects our hearers. Your understanding of the cultural scene will help you identify with your hearers.

The Religious Scene
This last decade of the twentieth century is a time of uncertainty for many. We have already seen that cultural values have changed, definitions of family are different, the pace of life is

hectic, the world is an unpredictable place. When life is uncertain and in flux, people often turn to religion for answers.

The growth of the New Age movement is the result of heightened sensitivity to spiritual concerns. The sale of popular books on spirituality and self-awareness, such as L. Ron Hubbard's *Dianetics,* is a sign that people are hungry to learn about spiritual realities. With this resurgence of interest, however, comes a peculiar down-side: people appear to be skeptical of traditional expressions of faith and mainline denominations. While interest in spirituality is increasing, interest in traditional denominations is declining rapidly.[7]

People moving into a community do not necessarily look for a church along denominational lines. Denominational loyalty is a thing of the past. If you assume that Methodists will come to your church because it's Methodist, or that Baptists will come to your church because it's the only Baptist church in town, you'd better be careful. People who expect quality in other aspects of their lives are less likely to join a church merely because it fits their denominational background.

People shop for churches today; they look for quality ministries and programs that meet their specific needs. Here are some questions people ask me: "What kind of youth program does your church have? Does your church offer a senior adult ministry? Do you have an after-school program for children?" I cannot remember that anyone has asked me about the denominational affiliation of the church.

The unchurched don't care about denominational programs and emphases. If they are persuaded to join a church, it's because of the quality of the worship service or the Bible teaching, because of the friendliness of the people, because the church met a physical need, or because the church has met their personal needs in some other way.

Once people accepted the church's authority and traditions without question. Today, fewer people are willing to follow traditions for tradition's sake. Many churches I have preached in during the past several years have a predominantly older membership. When I talk to their staffs about this phenomenon, they say that younger people just don't have time to get involved in all the programs of the church. I wonder whether that is the real reason. My guess is that younger people—people who have questioned institutional authority their whole lives—probably view the church as an archaic, obsolete institution. They find little relevance in the church's traditional programs.

If we are going to reach a broad spectrum of people in our communities, we must seek new models for doing ministry in a climate less friendly to our traditional boundaries. For example, moving beyond traditional lines is the key to the effectiveness of Willow Creek Community Church in South Barrington, Illinois. Bill Hybels, pastor there for sixteen years, has led the church in creating an environment that appeals to the unchurched. This nontraditional, nondenominational church ministers to fifteen thousand people every week. Willow Creek's method will not work in every setting, but what it tells us is that an understanding of the setting can help us design the appropriate ministry mix that's necessary to reach people.

The religions scene facing our churches presents major challenges to our preaching. We preach among people who are apathetic and mistrustful of traditional church authority. We preach to people who question the viability of the church in light of complex cultural realities. We preach to people who are disillusioned by the church's inability to make a tangible difference in the world. We must be aware of these factors if we are ever going to identify with the attitudes of our hearers. To disregard these issues is to create a great gulf of division between you and your hearers.

Analyzing These Scenes

Before we move to analyzing the congregational scene, we

should consider methods for evaluating the three scenes we have already addressed. Preachers are general practitioners who are eclectic in their interests and abilities. Most of us are not sociologists, and if we were, we would not have time to do the in-depth empirical research required of social scientists. But, as preachers, we are students of life; therefore, the analysis of our world and its cultural and religious scenes becomes a natural part of our lives.

Pay attention to the events that shape our world, and evaluate these events in terms of their impact—theologically, economically, politically, socially—on all of us. Develop a hermeneutical eye for interpreting events in the same way that you interpret biblical texts. We all watched the Berlin Wall come down. As that was happening, we should have asked ourselves questions like these: Since the breaking down of barriers has theological importance in the Bible, will the collapse of the Berlin Wall have theological significance in the world? How will world economic realities change because of this event? Does this event mean that we are on the brink of major political reshuffling? What kind of world will we have when the wall is gone? Whether the events are international, national or local, approach them with an inquisitive, probing curiosity.

Read widely with the same inquisitiveness. Read a local newspaper daily. This habit will give you a general overview of what is going on around the world. If there is a story of special interest, you can pursue it in depth. You should also read a newspaper that specializes in analyzing the world scene. *The New York Times, The Washington Post* or *The Wall Street Journal* should be a part of your weekly reading regimen.

Read books that provide portraits of contemporary life. *The Next Century* by David Halberstam, *Belonging in America* by Constance Perin, Neal Postman's *Amusing Ourselves to Death,* Alex Kotlowitz's *There Are No Children Here* and *Habits of the Heart* by Robert Bellah and colleagues are examples of books that provide informative portrayals of life in the twentieth century. Read books that focus on interpreting the role of religion in society today. Books like Robert Wuthnow's *The Restructuring of American Religion,* Garry Wills's *Under God: Religion and American Politics* and Quentin Schultze's *American Evangelicals and the Mass Media* shed interesting light on America's religious life. Subscribe to at least one journal or periodical that deals with the role of Christianity in modern culture. Take stock of the films that are playing at local theaters. Films often reflect the values and concerns of society. What are the theological implications of films such as *Driving Miss Daisy, Dead Poets Society* and *Mississippi Burning?*

Just as physicians and surgeons must continually read about advances in medical science, preachers must continually become informed about the world that shapes and is shaped by their preaching. Become an effective interpreter of the world by keeping yourself informed.

I can hear some of you saying, "What you ask us to do is impossible. There's just not enough time in the week to do all this reading and analysis. I don't have time to read anything as it is." My response is, you really don't have a choice if you are going to preach effectively to a contemporary congregation. Your daily church work does demand time and energy. But to be both prophet and priest to your people, you must be willing to be a student of the Bible and of life. Your preaching is most effective when you shine the light of the gospel onto the confusing paths on which your people walk. Help them discover that the message of Jesus Christ is as relevant today as it was in the first century.

The Congregational Scene
In the broadest sense, congregations are made up of people who gather for worship and religious instruction. A congregation is a complex social group centered on mutual religious

convictions and faith. There is more than a tacit kinship understood among the members of a congregation. By intentional
choice, they have banded together for fellowship, worship,
the celebration of traditional rituals, mutual caring and ministry
to those outside their group. It is to a congregation that we
preach.

In this book, I have used the terms *hearers* and *congregation*
interchangeably. I have attempted to avoid using the term *audience* to refer to the congregation. Moviegoers are an audience. When we sit in a movie theater, we may be of the same
economic level and live in the same neighborhood as others
in the audience. Our children may attend the same schools. We
may face the same social concerns as the people sitting next to
us. We may laugh or cry together during the movie because it
evokes emotions about the shared realities of our lives. But we
are not a congregation. When the movie ends, we depart our
separate ways. The connection made by the film event is over.
We are still a part of the same society, but the temporal relationship as audience has ended.

We address our preaching to a *congregation*. A congregation
has a shared sense of commitment. Through the ritual of baptism, the congregation identifies itself with the death and resurrection of Jesus Christ (Rom 6), and through Christ it is a part
of the universal church. The celebration of the Lord's Supper
also creates a sense of community as the congregation gathers
around the table for proclamation, fellowship and service.
When we preach, we preach to a congregation.

Therefore, the question asked by some homileticians today
is, Do you address your sermons to the congregation, as though
the congregation were a single-minded entity with a personality
all its own? Or do you view the congregation as a group of
individuals and address your sermons to the concerns specific
members bring with them to worship? If we are honest, we'll
probably answer yes to both questions.

The Congregation as a Social Group

We talk about a congregation as though it were a person and had a personality. If the sermon did not go well, we might say, "The congregation sure was lifeless today." Or, if things went well, we would probably shout: "Did you sense the congregation's excitement today?" You have probably heard people say, "That's an unfriendly congregation." Or, "That congregation is warm and loving." These statements personify the congregation as a single entity.

In our preaching we often consider the congregation as a social unit and deal with issues that face this personified group. Through a stewardship sermon we encourage the congregation to rethink giving patterns. We preach a sermon titled "Dreaming New Dreams" to encourage the congregation to think about a new vision for the future. In these cases, we are not dealing with the individuals that make up the congregation as much as we are speaking to the congregation's identity as a unified group. We are addressing the social consciousness of the congregation.

Every congregation comes to worship with a composite set of attitudes. Every congregation has a style, a particular behavior, a way of doing things. Every congregation displays certain values and outlooks toward the religious, cultural and world scenes of which it is a part. Burke calls these attitudes "frames of acceptance" and "frames of rejection" that are norms of experience held by the congregation.[8]

Frames of acceptance include the views of life accepted as normal for a particular social group; obviously, frames of rejection are the norms of behavior and experience that the group rejects. Frames of acceptance and rejection mirror the congregation's behavior and attitudes. By understanding these norms, you will know what your congregation considers acceptable or unacceptable behavior.

To preach a sermon on loving your enemies, you need to

know who the congregation's enemies are. A sermon on the
need for renewed faith might require you to discover the
frames of acceptance and rejection the congregation has about
faith. What ideas about faith does the congregation accept?
How does it define faith? Knowledge of the congregation's attitudes toward ideas, people and things is vital if you are going
to identify with them. If you fail to recognize what the congregation accepts or rejects, walls of resistance rather then identification are built in the communication process. You must get
to know the congregation, to empathize with them, to learn
their likes and dislikes, so you can figure out what they accept
and reject.

As preachers, we learn these frames in several ways. One is
by intentional inquiry. You might ask key church leaders pointed questions: How does this congregation view itself theologically? Is it liberal or conservative? What is its attitude toward
the poor? How do the members relate to minorities in the
community? We also learn the congregation's frames of acceptance and rejection by experience, during casual conversations
and, to an extent, intuitively as we minister. Some of this
happens as we become familiar with the congregation's vocabulary. How we talk about things and the names we give to
people and groups often reveal our attitudes about them.

If you want to know how your congregation feels about minorities, pay close attention to the names people use when
speaking about them. If a congregation abhors the use of al-
coholic beverages, you may hear its people speak of an alco-
holic as a "drunken bum." The term *drunken bum* reveals a
strong sentiment about the use of alcohol—obviously a frame
of rejection.

Learning a congregation's attitudes toward people, institutions and issues is a key step toward identifying with it. This
does not mean that you have to agree with members' attitudes
or accept their frames of acceptance and rejection. Often the

role of preaching is a catalyst to change a congregation's attitudes and behaviors. But analyzing a congregation in terms of their frames of acceptance and rejection is a key step in identifying with them.

The Congregation as a Collection of Individuals

We also preach with individuals in mind. If several members in the congregation have recently lost loved ones, we don't consider grief in an abstract sense as we prepare sermons. While grief is a universal emotion, our sermon on grief moves from the general to the particular because of our sensitivity to the bereaved persons in the congregation. Similarly, when preaching on issues surrounding aging, we will be most effective when we consider the actual questions and struggles the members of this congregation ask, feel and experience in their older years.

When we preach, we address congregations as social groups; we also address them by dealing with issues facing individuals. Our best preaching, preaching that identifies with people, happens when we understand the congregation as a group and when we get to know the lives of the individuals in our churches. Though these people are members of a group, perhaps even a homogeneous group, they still have different interests, knowledge, attitudes, desires and goals. When we put names and faces on the people sitting in front of us on Sunday morning, we are well on the road to identifying with them.

In the first chapter, we discussed the issue of identification and differences. You must be aware of the differences present within your congregation. Some of your listeners have been Christians for a long time; some are new converts. Their needs and understandings are very different. Do you take these differences into consideration when you prepare your sermons? Some who are present on a Sunday morning are not even members of the congregation. Perhaps they are seekers. Are your sermons clear enough that a nonbeliever could understand and respond? Do you use theological terms that only believers understand?

Some who are in worship are not there out of choice. Teenagers may be present by their parents' direct intervention. Some are in church merely to appease a demanding spouse. Some people seem to dare us to interest them by our preaching. Do you take these people into consideration when you preach?

I was a member of a church where the pastor preached evangelistic sermons exclusively. Few people ever responded to the sermons, because the congregation was made up primarily of believers. This preacher failed to analyze the congregation and its needs adequately. The people were starving for nurture from the pulpit; their needs were not being addressed with the evangelistic sermons they heard.

To prevent this from happening in your church, analyze the mix of religious belief, and make sure your preaching communicates at various points along the belief spectrum—from unbelievers to seekers to those who are attempting to become more effective disciples of Christ.

You should be aware of the general demographics of your congregation. A simple thing such as understanding differences between urban and rural people can drastically change your preaching. If a preacher who has been pastoring a rural congregation in the South accepts a call to a pastorate in Philadelphia or Boston, he or she will have to make major adjustments in pulpit ministry. Agricultural illustrations may be understandable to Northern industrialists, but they may not seem relevant. Urban and suburban people live a faster-paced life than rural people. People who live in the country expect the pastor to stop by the house, drink some iced tea and sit and chat for a while. City people often want to be left alone and would view this kind of pastoral visit as an intrusion.

Take the gender makeup of your congregation seriously.

Men and women have different needs and different ways of knowing and understanding. Do you take this into consideration when you prepare your sermons? For example, biblical images portray God with both feminine and masculine attributes. Does your preaching reflect that fact, inviting men, women, boys and girls to identify with God? Does your preaching show that all people have worth in God's eyes? I have heard sermons in which the preacher implied that women are somehow not equal to men, an opinion not supported by the Bible (Gen 1:26-27; Gal 3:28). Does your overall illustrative material create identification for all your hearers? For example, if you continually use sports illustrations that appeal only to men, you will not identify with the women. Women like sports too. What illustrations would appeal to both men and women?

An obvious but often overlooked issue in congregational analysis is the age mix of the congregation. Needs, concerns and issues are different in different periods of our lives. Young adults are concerned about achieving economic independence from their parents; middle-aged adults are paying their children's college expenses; older adults are adjusting to retirement income. Young adults are starting careers; median adults are developing second and sometimes third careers; older adults are making the best of more leisure time during retirement. Young adults are starting families; median adults are coping with teenagers, young adult children and the empty-nest syndrome; older adults enjoy being grandparents. Even these examples are too general and do not consider all the age groups in your church.

Know the occupations of your church members. Do they work weekends and nights? Are they manual laborers or white-collar workers? How do their occupations affect their outlook on life? You will also want to learn the socioeconomic makeup and educational level of the members of your congregation.

A caution I would raise about analyzing your congregation

is to take care that you avoid stereotyping the people. Even the examples I've offered are stereotypical. I provide them to provoke you to think about the specific issues that are present in your *particular* congregation.

Be a critical observer. Ask questions. When asking, ask openended questions. Too often we think we know the answers already, so our questions are off the mark. I once heard Detroit pastor Fred Sampson say, "When you ask the wrong questions, you begin the wrong quest." Learn to ask questions that inform you about the real needs of the real people to whom you preach. Spend time listening to them. Listen to how they talk about their financial worries, their dreams for their children and grandchildren, their concerns about the environment. Develop a listening ear as you mingle with them after church, as you eat with them during the fellowship meal, as you minister to them in the hospital.

The issues facing your congregation are real issues to which the Bible speaks. As a careful interpreter of the Bible and the world, you can show your hearers the connection between the two. A piece of advice attributed to Karl Barth says that preachers should preach with the Bible in one hand and a newspaper in the other. Not bad advice for us as we become one with our hearers.

Summing Up
Careful congregation analysis is the key to preaching through identification. When we know what our hearers go through and how the world in which they live affects them, we can minister to them through our sermons. As we preach, our congregations will appreciate our sensitivity in speaking out of the sincere relationship we have developed with them. In the next chapter, we will look at how to develop sermons that identify with the needs and issues of your hearers.

6/Strategies for Identification

Critical and imaginative works are answers to questions
posed by the situation in which they arose.
KENNETH BURKE,
THE PHILOSOPHY OF LITERARY FORM

*D*oes my preaching accomplish anything? Do my sermons
do anything in the lives of my hearers? Does my preaching
have any impact on the behavior and attitudes of my congregation? Is what I do through my preaching viable ministry, or
am I engaged in a futile practice that doesn't matter very much?
Could my time be better spent on other forms of ministry?

Do these questions sound familiar? At some point each of us
has wondered whether preaching is really worth the effort that
we put into it. How often have you worked hours on a sermon,
only to feel that it made no difference? We look for some
immediate effect from our preaching, something more than the
"Good sermon, Preacher" response that so often comes at the
foyer door. We do hope that the sermons we preach make some
difference in how our hearers face crises, how they make sense
out of financial dilemmas, how they interpret their daily situations in light of the gospel message. The question haunts us:
What does my preaching do?

In reality, we may never know the impact our sermons have
on the lives of our hearers. While in the Air Force, I visited a

church near the base. Having been reared in a tradition that did not emphasize proclamation, I was enthralled by how clearly the Bible could be communicated. The preaching I heard in my new church had a tremendous impact on my life. At that time I did not meet the pastor, not even to shake his hand.

Years later, we met. He was a trustee on the board of the seminary where I teach preaching. I told him of the impact his preaching had on my life and how it had influenced my decision to enter the ministry and pursue studies in preaching. He reminded me that so often we never know how our preaching affects our hearers. Yet we need to remember that preaching can and does influence lives.

Harry Emerson Fosdick made a statement that has influenced both my teaching and my practice of preaching:

> The preacher's business is not merely to discuss repentance but to persuade people to repent; not merely to debate the meaning and possibility of Christian faith, but to produce Christian faith in the lives of his listeners; not merely to talk about the available power of God to bring victory over trouble and temptation, but to send people from their worship on Sunday with victory in their possession.[1]

Preaching can do something!

The goal of this chapter is to use identification in exploring how to design sermons strategically so they will have an impact on your hearers. I use the words *strategy* and *strategic* to show my concern that preachers write or compose sermons with a stated purpose in mind. If you are uncomfortable with the idea of sermon strategies, find a synonym that connotes an *intentional* design. The key is intentionality.

Perhaps our preaching does not seem to do anything because it is missing the intentional element. In the previous chapter, we focused on getting to know your congregation and their needs. Sermons that you strategically compose address your hearers where they live, work and play.

A picture is worth a thousand words. Allow me the freedom to embellish "Nathan's Parable" a bit. Nathan faced a terrible problem. He had to preach a sermon to King David that would persuade the king that he had been disobedient to God. Nathan went to his study and tried to design a sermon that would evoke a response from King David. He remembered from a homiletics course the formula for one type of sermon: "Tell them what you're going to tell them; tell them; and then tell them what you've told them." As Nathan pondered his preaching task, he became uncomfortable about going to the king with such a sermon outline. He figured that after he told David "what he was going to tell him"—God is displeased with you—the sermon would end there; he would be looking for another place to preach!

Pacing his study frantically, Nathan agonized about how to preach the message he had for the king. He would rush to his desk and jot down what seemed to be a wonderful idea, only to realize that it wouldn't work. He crumpled one piece of paper after another, until the floor was strewn with erstwhile sermon ideas. But after what seemed an endless time, he had an idea that really *was* wonderful.

When it was time to preach, Nathan went to the king and began: "There were two men in a certain town. One was rich and the other poor. The rich man had many sheep and cattle; the poor man had only one little lamb. He raised this lamb and it grew up with him and his children. The man loved the lamb so much that he treated it like one of his children.

"Now a traveler came to the rich man, and the rich man wanted to honor his visitor with a feast. But he was not willing to prepare one of his animals for the feast, so he took the poor man's pet lamb and prepared a meal for his guest with it."

When David heard the sermon, he was furious and said to Nathan, "As surely as the LORD lives, the man who did this deserves to die! He must pay for that lamb four times over, because he did such a thing and had no pity."² Then Nathan, in the evangelical tradition, offered the invitation hymn "Just As I Am." The sermon jarred David; Nathan had made his point.

Nathan received a hearing from the king because he developed a sermon strategy that penetrated the king's defenses. Nathan did not point a finger and shout or become angry. David heard the sermon and indicted himself—a brilliant strategy on Nathan's part.

Sermons strategically composed address the hearers where they are. They reflect a purpose and an intent for our preaching.

Chapter one introduced the idea of strategies for identification. Using Kenneth Burke's ideas, we noted that one way to look at sermons is to consider them as strategic answers to the questions being posed by the situation in which they were written or preached. In the example of Nathan and David, we can assume some questions that the situation posed: In light of all the good things the Lord had given David, why did David "despise the word of the LORD by doing what is evil" in God's eyes (2 Sam 12:7-9)? How would one confront the king with his sin? What kind of message, in form and content, would be a transforming word for King David? Nathan's sermon, or parable as we traditionally call it, answered these questions.

The life situations of our hearers are always posing questions. Sometimes these questions are explicit. A teenager asks, "How can I be a Christian in school, where peer pressure is so hard to handle?" A single parent asks, "The Bible portrays the ideal family as a husband, a wife and children. That's not my situation. Does the Christian faith speak to my circumstances?" A recent college graduate asks, "I have career choices to make. Both positions are excellent, but each has its down-side. Which position should I take?" A widow asks, "My husband and I planned our whole lives for our retirement, and now he's gone. How am I going to make it without him?"

Sometimes the questions posed by the situation are more general and implicit: What does it mean to be a disciple of Christ? How can faith in Christ be transformed into practice in the marketplace? If God is a loving God, why is there evil in the world?

The situations in which you and I preach are always whispering these questions and others like them. Remember, none of us preaches in a vacuum. Either explicitly or implicitly, the context in which we preach has an effect on our preaching. If our preaching is to be relevant, it must take these questions seriously.

Burke felt that newspaper editorials, plays, songs and speeches were strategic answers to questions being posed by the situation in which they arose. In Christian preaching, sermons are sometimes answers to questions the Bible poses to situations. As preachers we might ask: What biblical text addresses this particular situation? What need, problem or concern of the congregation does this text address? Where is the point of contact between the congregation's situation and the biblical text? What questions does the text pose to us?

For example, in the Sermon on the Mount, Jesus said: "You have heard that it was said, 'You shall love your neighbor and hate your enemy.' But I say to you, Love your enemies and pray for those who persecute you, so that you may be children of your Father in heaven" (Mt 5:43-45). What questions does this passage pose to your congregation? Who are the enemies Jesus challenges us to love? How is it possible to love and pray for people who are persecuting us? How do we practice loving our enemies?

Whether the questions are posed by a biblical text or by the congregation's situation, the key is that we focus on the particular rather than the general. For example, consider the crisis caused by the death of a young child to cancer. Questions emerge because of this tragedy: Why would God allow a child to die? Why did a child within our congregation come down with cancer? We prayed that God would heal this child, but God did not answer our prayer; why not? Notice how specific these questions are. Sermon strategies that connect with the life situations of your hearers deal with their particular situations.

The Strategy of Attitude

The task of preaching presumes faithful exegesis of a passage of Scripture. Once you have arrived at the message of the biblical text, you begin making decisions about how you will communicate the message. What will the sermon look like? At this point you are much like a sculptor facing a large piece of marble. You basically know what you want to create, but you are not sure how to go about it or exactly how the final work will look. You must now make some strategic decisions.

While you could approach the piece of marble from any side at this early stage, it's probably good to begin by deciding on your point of view. What is my attitude about the message I'm going to proclaim? What stance am I taking on the subject? Is my role as preacher to be an adversarial one? Am I going to communicate through my sermon that I am a proponent of a certain position? If the biblical message deals with the church's response to the poor, is my stance one of opposing oppressive systems or one of acting as an advocate for the poor?

One definition of good preaching is that it comforts the afflicted and afflicts the comfortable. Comforting the afflicted requires the stance of a priest; afflicting the comfortable calls for the stance of a prophet. As you preach week after week, being faithful to the biblical witness and to your call as preacher, you will preach from one of these two stances, or some combination of them.

An example might help. In the following sermon introduc-

tion, my strategy was to create identification with my congregation by sounding as though I were standing against the subject.
I preached the sermon, based on 2 Corinthians 8:1-5, on Stewardship Sunday:

Oh, how do I begin this one? For a year and four months
I have been able to put it off. Why should I be so reluctant
to deal with a subject that is such a central part of biblical
faith? Maybe the reason I am so reluctant to preach about
it is because sermons dealing with money and the need for
money in the church were so much a part of what I remember preaching to be as I grew up in the church. Every
sermon seemed to deal with money: more money for this
project or more money for that building. All I ever heard was
money, money, money! That's why I stopped going to church
as a young person; I got tired of hearing that preached every
week. Maybe the indictment "all they ever preached was
money" was nothing more than a good excuse for never
going to church: "Why should I go? All he ever talks about
is money!"

I'm sure that background colors my reluctance about
preaching a sermon on giving. I don't want to give anyone
the excuse that I always used for never going to church. I
don't want to deal with a subject that would make you feel
too uncomfortable. I want everyone to like my sermons and
to like me, and one rule in the "if-you-want-them-to-like-you
department" is *never* preach about money. Let their con-
science be their guide.

Maybe the reason I am reluctant to preach about giving
is all the negative comments I hear from people about TV
ministers and their incessant pleas for money. Over and
over, I have heard people say, "All those TV preachers are
doing is getting rich. They preach the gospel out of one side
of their mouths and ask for money out of the other side."
That critique causes me to approach the subject carefully.

God forbid that a sermon I preach about giving would actually cause someone to close their ears to the gospel.

While these two explanations might help to explain my reluctance, they still do not answer my original question, "How do I begin this one?" I thought about beginning this sermon by telling the story about how one pastor began one of his Stewardship Day Sermons: "I have done something this week which I have never before done in all the years of my ministry as a pastor—and something which I hope I will never have to do again." He paused, then he began again, "I took the stewardship records into my office, and one by one, I looked over them and studied them very carefully. And as I did this, a marvelous revelation occurred to me. I have been listening to the wrong people! Those who do most of the squawking around here are not making enough investment in the church to squawk about anything. And those who are giving the most, I never hear from, unless it is time for prayer."

Now that's a pretty bold way to begin a sermon on stewardship, but I decided not to use that story because I felt it was too bold as an introduction to my first stewardship sermon with you. Then I came across the story about a minister who spoke as a guest preacher in a small country church. He was accompanied by his little son. After the worship service, the minister recalled that no offering had been taken, and, as he was in the habit of never going to the Lord's house without presenting an offering, he left a dollar bill in the offering box beside the door. As he and his son walked away from the church, one of the members came running after them, saying, "It is our custom here to give to the visiting preacher whatever we find in the offering box after the service." The member handed to the minister the dollar bill he himself had left there. They started to walk off again, and the little boy looked at his father and said, "Dad, if you had given more, you would have gotten more, wouldn't you?"

While that story does say a lot, I didn't want to use it because it implies that giving should be conditioned by what we will get in return, and that is not biblical, and is not a proper Christian motive for giving.

In this sermon introduction, my stance was to identify explicitly with the concerns and issues of the congregation. By showing them that I had the same negative feelings about stewardship sermons that they had, and by sharing my struggle about even beginning a stewardship sermon, I identified, strategically, with my hearers.

If you anticipate resistance to your subject, you will make certain decisions about your stance. In the above example of the stewardship sermon, I decided to reduce the resistance by identifying some of my apprehension about preaching stewardship sermons as well as about hearing them. Through the use of personal testimony and humor, I identified with the hearers, their resistance was lowered, their interest was piqued and they were willing to give me a hearing on a possibly controversial subject. The responses I heard following the sermon suggested that the strategy I chose had been effective.

If you are preaching a text in which you are taking the stance of prophet, you will probably want to think about resistance that you must overcome. If you are preaching a text in which you take the stance of priest, you may find that you have other strategic decisions to make. Chances are, in this second case, that you will not have overt resistance to overcome; your enemy may be apathy or complacency.

This is especially true when you are preaching from a familiar passage of Scripture. Most congregations have heard many sermons on Luke 15:11-32. Following a revival service at which the preacher preached on this passage, one of the older church members said to me, "I only wish that younger son had had a dog. Then we could at least hear something different about the prodigal son. I really don't care if I ever hear another sermon about him again." This sounds like a rather harsh indictment, but his point is well taken.

When this man came to church and saw the text in the bulletin, he probably decided right then that he would not listen to the sermon. Now, whether we like it or not, we all have parishioners in our congregations who think like this man when they discover that you're preaching on a familiar text. They believe they have heard it all before, there is nothing new to be heard, and they are barely willing to sit and tolerate another sermon on that text.

What strategy will you use to begin a sermon on a familiar text? Imagine how the man who was tired of the prodigal son would respond if you began this way:

I am so tired of hearing about the prodigal son. In my lifetime I have heard at least 859 sermons on this text, and out of those 859, 32 were my own sermons. I couldn't care less if I ever heard about him again. But lo and behold, I'm looking at the lectionary text for today, and guess what it is? That's right, Luke 15, that prodigal son again. We already know everything there is to know about this kid. What more can be said?

You may get more agreement with this kind of introduction strategy than you bargained for. You have created identification with your hearers' concerns, and you now have their attention. The strategy has worked.

The Strategy of Interest

In his book *The Empty Pulpit,* Clyde Reid lists seven common criticisms of contemporary preaching. One criticism on the list is "Most sermons today are dull, boring, and uninteresting."[3] That is a sad indictment of preaching. People do not, or at least should not, come to church to be entertained; yet that doesn't mean that what they hear in our sermons need not be inter-

esting. People pay attention when what they hear is interesting
to them, when they sense that the sermon has import for their
lives.

Kenneth Burke offers a humorous anecdote about the importance of interest in communication: "It is not hard to imagine that if a grasshopper could speak he would be much more
readily interested in what you had to tell him about 'Birds That
Eat Grasshoppers' than in a more scholarly and better presented talk on 'Mating Habits of the Australian Auk.' "[4]

While it may come as a surprise to us, our listeners are not
really interested in "the eschatological implications of the parousia." For one thing, they don't have the foggiest notion what
that means. For another, they are not living experientially in
the *eschaton*—that is, the last days. Now I am not going to argue
about whether we are or are not in the last days. The key for
us to realize is that our people are experientially living in the
here and now: they go to work and face pressures on the job;
they go to school and face pressures there; they are making
career decisions; they are troubled by the death of a loved one;
they are helping their teenager cope with the changes of ad-
olescence; their checkbook does not balance; they have an
unexpected doctor's bill; the car needs a new muffler and the
insurance is due; they want to spend more time with their families. The list could go on ad infinitum. As we saw in the last
chapter, this list describes where our congregations live and
work and have their being. If your preaching intersects their
lives at these places, Reid's indictment will not apply to your
preaching because you will be interesting.

How do we make our sermons interesting? Keeping our
hearers in mind at every step of our sermon preparation is the
starting place. From the point of selecting a text, through the
interpretation of that text, to the composition and delivery of
the sermon, have your hearers in your mind's eye. By remem-
bering who they are, you will be well on the way to identifying

with them and making your sermons interesting.

The selection of supporting materials, such as stories and illustrations, is a strategy for creating interest and identification. Illustrations that are contemporary create more interest than dated illustrations. While there are some good stories in books of illustrations, I have found that they do not have the interest factor of those taken from contemporary situations and the lives of the preacher and the congregation. Stories from your life and the lives of your parishioners, when used properly, make interesting illustrations.

Once preachers culled great literature for sermon illustrations. Unfortunately, our congregations, by and large, are not familiar with literature. To use literature effectively in illustrations, you must be creative. Our hearers are much more familiar with contemporary films and television programs. Films like *The Trip to Bountiful, Driving Miss Daisy* and *Dead Poets Society* have tremendous interest potential for sermon illustrations. Many people in your congregation have watched "The Cosby Show," "Roseanne," "The Simpsons" and reruns of "M*A*S*H." Illustrations drawn from these sources will quickly create identification and interest appeal.

You may be thinking, "I don't watch those kinds of TV programs." That may be the case, but chances are your people do, and you are attempting to get them to listen to your sermons. Having done effective congregational analysis, you will know what your people listen to, watch and read. That tells you where their interests lie.

The local newspaper is another source for interesting illustrations because it contains news directly related to your congregation's lives. Local political issues are of interest to your hearers; high school and college sports news can provide contemporary illustrations; the newspaper always has human interest stories of which your hearers are familiar. The question you must continually ask yourself is, Will this be interesting to my hearers?

A word of caution is needed here. There is always a danger that a preacher's zeal to be interesting can get out of control. We have all heard sermons in which the biblical message is lost in the maze of interesting stories and anecdotes. Illustrations are to be used as servants of the message. When the illustration begins to take charge, the sermon is in trouble.

Another caution is to vary the source of your illustrations. I had a student who loved "The Andy Griffith Show." In the first sermon he preached in class, he drew three of four illustrations from that show. The illustrations were creative and interesting, and they illustrated the point of the sermon. When he preached his second sermon, to our surprise, the introduction and the conclusion were stories from "Andy Griffith." His fellow students insightfully suggested that his congregation might not be as enamored with Andy, Barney and Opie as he was. His third sermon only cited Aunt Bee once.

The class's critique was on target. Be careful that you do not overuse one particular source of illustrative material, no matter how interesting or relevant to the subject it may be. Keep your sermons fresh and interesting by citing a variety of support materials.

The list of contemporary and interesting sources for sermon illustrations could go on: children's books, popular literature, popular songs, familiar hymns. The interesting preacher always has his or her eyes wide open, looking for illustrations that make sermons come alive. Remember our friend the grasshopper!

Don't be afraid to use your imagination for creating interesting sermons. Nathan's parable and the introduction to my stewardship sermon exemplify two very different approaches, but both relied heavily on the preacher's imagination.

Allow your mind some room to imagine by giving yourself enough preparation time. I find that my imagination shuts down when I put my mind on a rigid deadline. Telling myself

"Okay, now be creative! I've got to get this sermon written" has never worked for me. Early in the week, I sit down with a note pad, clear my mind and begin thinking about how I can write an interesting sermon on the text at hand. As ideas begin to come, whether rapidly or slowly, I jot them down. After a while, if no ideas come, I may make a hospital visit or work on some administrative tasks, but incubating in the back of my mind is Sunday's sermon. Before too long, I am amazed at how ideas begin to flow. Some of the ideas are good, some are bad, but all are worth considering.

In preaching, we must allow our God-given imagination the freedom to develop. Interesting sermons grow out of the richness of our ability to imagine.

Interest in preaching is never for interest's sake. It is always for the sake of identifying with the audience, saying to them that we have their best interests at heart and that our preaching is with them rather than at them. Interesting sermons do something.

The Strategy of Form

Communication depends not only on the content of the message but also on the form the message takes. This statement does not imply that form takes precedence over content; but in preaching, we must not separate the two. The strategy of form asks the following questions: What will the sermon look like? Will it take a traditional deductive form based on points to be communicated? Will I, like Nathan, develop a narrative strategy to carry the message? How will I get into the sermon? What will I say in the introduction? Where will I move from there? How will I conclude the sermon? The answers to these questions are the basis for the strategy of sermon form.

If the purpose of the sermon is to teach a doctrine, the most effective form may follow a structured outline. This form offers a thesis—that is, the message of the sermon—and then logically presents the points to be taught. Typically, point one needs to be understood before point two, and point two is the basis for point three, and so on. This strategy flows from a concern that the congregation understands the relationships among the points and remembers them. When a sermon's purpose is to teach, this type of deductive form is perhaps the best. It lends itself to easy retention.

If the purpose of a sermon is to persuade the hearers to taking a specific action or changing their attitudes, the deductive form may not be best because it seldom leaves room for surprise or irony. Nathan's parable is again a good example. Sometimes we want our hearers to have an experience with God during the preaching, and we are not as interested that they remember the details of the sermon when they leave the church. Specifying our goals helps us establish the form for our sermons.

In biblical preaching, we hope that the sermon will do in the lives of our hearers what the biblical text did and does in the lives of its readers. Therefore, we may allow the form of the text to suggest the form of the sermon. If the text is a narrative, perhaps its meaning will be communicated best through a narrative form. A sample sermon in the next chapter uses a narrative form that corresponds to the form of the text. Poetic texts, which are rich in metaphor and parallelism, may suggest a sermon form that leans heavily on these characteristics. An epistle that has a salutation, a blessing, the message and then a final blessing may suggest the form that a sermon on that epistle should take. Since the Bible comes to us as form and substance, we should rely on biblical forms to help us communicate our message.

No matter what particular form you choose, there are several elements that should characterize all forms. The first of these is unity. There is no quicker way to lose a congregation's interest than to preach a sermon that does not hang together. As you compose the sermon, you should continually refer to the message you arrived at when interpreting the text. Keeping that in front of you, and keeping the sermon's purpose in mind, will prevent you from chasing the proverbial rabbit.

Unity does not mean that you cannot develop a subject or draw from a variety of sources besides the Bible for illustrative material. It does mean that this sermon is a particular message with a particular purpose. It has a unified focus.

A second characteristic of sermon form is movement. The hearers should have a sense that the sermon is going somewhere. Don't give them a reason for complaining, "She kept repeating herself. The sermon never went anywhere." This doesn't mean your hearers always have to know where you are going. David did not know where Nathan was going, but he knew he was going somewhere.

The easiest way to create movement in a sermon is to use a narrative form. Notice how Jesus' preaching relied heavily on story and parable. Eugene Lowry encourages preachers to think of plotting a sermon rather than outlining a sermon.[5] An outline, by its nature, is a vertical structure and, like all vertical structures, not naturally prone to movement, while a sermon based on narrative form has movement naturally built in.

However, even sermons based on deductive outlines can have well-developed movement. As you compose the outline, avoid asking yourself, What is the next point? Instead, ask, How do I move to the next thing that must be said? You will create identification in an implicit way because your hearers appreciate your concern for preaching sermons that go somewhere and say something.

The third characteristic is that the sermon form serves the purpose of the sermon. The form that a sermon takes is integrally related to purpose. Ask yourself, What is the purpose of this sermon? Or ask the question in several different ways for clarification: What do I want to accomplish with this sermon? As a result of hearing this sermon, what do I want my hearers to do, feel or experience? If the congregation took this sermon seriously, what would they do?

Sermons should have behavioral objectives. From my first class that I took in preaching, I can still remember my professor's "key" question: "So what?" When a congregation finishes hearing one of your sermons, can they answer the "so what" question? One of my colleagues pointed out that the "what" question addressed to the sermon deals with information: What was the sermon about? The "so what" question is interested in transformation: Having heard this sermon, are the hearers not only informed but also transformed?

The sermon's form should enhance the purpose of the sermon. For example, the arrangement of material may help carry out your purpose. In an example sermon that appears in chapter seven, I decided to tell part of a story in the introduction and conclude the story in the conclusion. I made this decision based on what I hoped to achieve with the sermon—that was, helping hearers to understand that God promises to be present even when his presence is not detectable.

A final characteristic of form is proportion. That means that you should take more time dealing with important matters and less time dealing with matters of little importance. The introduction of the sermon should not be eighteen minutes long and the body of the sermon two minutes. Such a sermon would be out of proportion.

The form the sermon takes is an important strategic decision you must make. Varying forms will help you keep your hearers' interest. Allow the form of the sermon to develop naturally through a composition process. You should always be willing to adjust the form of the sermon as it develops and matures. Remember that the sermon's form is servant to your purpose.

The Strategy of Language
For those preachers who write a full sermon manuscript before

they preach, the strategy of language is probably a step of the revision stage. Others compose their sermons orally, preaching from notes. Whatever method you use, you must be aware that one of the most effective ways of creating identification with your hearers is the language you use in the sermon. If your sermons are strewn with technical terms and theological jargon that you heard in the seminary classroom, you will probably receive low marks for identification in the typical church setting.

The strategy of language is saying the right thing in the right way.[6] Through your particular style of language, by identifying your style with theirs, you communicate identification to a congregation. Saying the right thing is not placating the congregation, but is enabling identification to take place between you and your hearers.

A formal style filled with theological language may be right for communicating with a congregation made up of professional people. However, that same style may be totally inappropriate for a congregation in a blue-collar neighborhood. And using overly simplistic language in a congregation made up of professors would be as ineffective as using a formal style in a congregation of manual laborers.

A sermon's style should have the characteristics of oral rather than written language, because preaching is an oral event. A sermon's language needs to be simple without being condescending. The language you use should be clear and interesting, inviting the congregation to listen, enabling the congregation to identify with your message rather than rejecting it because the language is offensive to them. Raymond Bailey insightfully points out that "style is concerned with more than words. The phrase, clause, and paragraph are of equal or greater importance than word choice. The combination of words determines effect."[7]

If you want to identify with your congregation, you should be aware of the language that the people commonly use. A vocabulary selected with your particular hearers in mind contains words that will identify you with them. Always review your sermons, either in manuscript or on a tape, looking for places where your language could be better crafted to enable understanding and identification.

The language you use when you preach is one of the most important factors for creating identification. In chapter four I mentioned the importance of using inclusive language. Again, as a strategic decision, your language should include and invite all your hearers to be active participants in the preaching event.

Summing Up
Good sermons do not just happen. Preachers create effective sermons through hard work, prayerful meditation, creative imagination and intentional strategies. In this chapter I have suggested ways you can deliberately compose sermons that identify with your congregation. The next chapter contains three sermons that model effective identification in preaching.

7/Sample Sermons

*I*n this chapter, I present three sermons that model identification in preaching. Two are sermons I have preached, and one is a sermon written and preached by one of my students.

As you read the sermons, think about the issues that have been raised throughout the book. I've provided reflection and analysis of the first sermon for you; I give questions at the end of the chapter to guide you through the analysis of the other two. Read the sermons with a critical eye, to learn from their strengths and weaknesses. Then I suggest you reflect on your sermons, evaluating them to see whether they intersect the life experiences of your hearers. Ask yourself, Does this sermon reflect a sensitivity to *these* hearers? Does this sermon address a need faced by the people of *this congregation now?* Have I identified with *them?*

What Do You Do When You Find Jesus Asleep?
Mark 4:35-41

I preached this sermon when I was pastor of Evergreen Baptist Church in Frankfort, Kentucky, a semirural community near the state capital.

The congregation consisted of all age groups, with a large percentage of senior adults and a balance between median and young adults. There were children and youth in the congregation. Traditional families, single-parent families, some single adults, and some widows and widowers were present. Many members had grown up in the church. Their families, going back two or three generations, have been church members. The congregation was solidly middle-class, conservative politically and moderate theologically. The fact that many members worked for state government often colored their outlook on issues. Many people had farms; some grew tobacco and others had small herds of cattle. Most of the farmers, however, did not make their living by farming.

The folks of Evergreen considered themselves a "typical" Southern Baptist church. Obviously, I can picture their faces; you must use your imagination as you read the sermon, which was part of a series of sermons on Mark's Gospel.

One moment they were flying as high as any couple could. The next moment was darker than any darkness they had ever experienced. The couple had so desperately wanted to have a family, and had been so full of excitement when they found out that they were going to have another child.

The day Karen was born was special; now they had a son and a daughter. Her skin was so soft and smooth to the touch. With rosy red cheeks and beautiful deep blue eyes, she seemed so full of life that the parents could hardly believe their ears when the doctor came and said to them, "Unless Karen is given a blood transfusion immediately, she will not live."

Can you imagine how the parents felt? They were frightened, anxious, wondering what the transfusion was all about, whether it was the right thing to do. They consented to go ahead with the transfusion. Then again, they were unable to believe their ears when the doctor came and said, "I'm sorry, we've done all we can do." Shortly after that, Karen died. Her mother in anger, rage and frustration cried out, "Where is God when you need him?"

What do we do when we find Jesus asleep? That is the question the young parents were asking. And that's the question the disciples were asking. It had started out as a great day. They were going to take Jesus to the other side of the lake, but on the way suddenly the winds blew up and a storm started to rage. Before they knew it, the boat started to fill with water, and they became extremely frightened and concerned. Not only did the storm concern them, but they were concerned that Jesus didn't seem to care. "Don't you care if we drown?" they asked. But he was *asleep!*

What do you do when you find Jesus asleep? That is the profound question when crisis comes to all our lives. When despair impinges itself upon us, we wonder that same thing. It becomes the question when a parent finds out that he or she has cancer and the prognosis is not good. It is what happens when your boss tells you that the company's contract is going to end, and you're going to be laid off. You wonder how you are ever going to buy food, let alone pay the rent. It is the question asked when the relationship "made in heaven" ends.

It is hard to understand. One moment everything is going great; the next moment the storm of crisis begins to blow, and your whole world sinks around you. In anger and fear and frustration we cry out to God, "Don't you care? Don't you care that we are perishing? Don't you care that our lives are collapsing around us?" How do we deal with those moments of crisis, those moments of despair, that bring anger and frustration and hurt? We're concerned not only because our ship is sinking, but also because it seems as though God doesn't care.

What do you do when you find Jesus asleep? That is the question of despair raised by the disciples, by the parents of little Karen, by the parents of a teenager who is out of control, by the patient who hears that the tumor is malignant, by the family finding it difficult to make ends meet, by the woman whose husband dies just as the two of them had begun to enjoy their long-anticipated retirement. That is the question when a friendship is lost because of a foolish fight, when a marriage falls apart because the two cannot communicate, when that first young love is devastated by a breakup. "Do you not care?" He's *asleep* in the boat! What do you do when you find Jesus asleep?

The text provides some answers for us, perhaps, but more than that, it points out some problems, common problems, that seem to come whenever and wherever there is crisis. To begin, notice that the storm came suddenly. Now the disciples knew that could happen. They were extremely familiar with this waterway. They realized that at any moment a squall could erupt out of the horizon and spread itself quickly across the water. They knew that could happen, but it didn't make it any easier to deal with when it did.

My family and I own a 1977 AMC Gremlin. That's not an animal, that's a car. We bought it new in Fort Lauderdale, Florida, in 1977 and have had it ever since. It runs pretty well. Occasionally it has some problems. Last year in the wintertime, it was my first opportunity to teach at the seminary as a contract instructor. I was so looking forward to the first day I would go to class. I'm one for punctuality, so on the first day of class I got up early, about five o'clock in the morning, and realized that it was pouring rain. I was getting ready to leave the house around six o'clock and my wife said to me, "Do you want to take the 'better' car?" (We do have a "better" car!) I said, "No, that's okay. I'll take the Gremlin, no problem."

I got in the Gremlin and drove about two miles; then it started to sputter. There seemed to be a kind of vapor lock, so that when I pressed the gas pedal nothing happened. I backed off the gas pedal, and lo and behold, the engine started up again. I thought, "Everything is going to be fine." So I got onto the expressway to drive from Frankfort to Louisville, about a thirty-eight-mile trip. When I got onto the expressway, I began to have trouble with the car again.

I couldn't get the car to go above twenty-five miles per hour. It was about six a.m. and all the truckers were on the road. Trucks don't have a whole lot of respect for Gremlins. As I drove down the road, doing a great twenty-five to thirty miles an hour, the trucks were whipping around me, the rain was pouring down, and I was frustrated as I looked at my watch. It was now a quarter past six; I thought I'd surely be late. It was one of those points of no return. Should I turn around and get the other car, or should I press on?

I said to myself, "Well, everybody's always talking about taking a step of faith, so press on." And I did, and I got nowhere. I would head up a hill, and the Gremlin would just about make it up the hill and then would stall. You don't realize there are any hills between Frankfort and Louisville until you have to drive up one in a car that won't run. I was driving up the hills and having all kinds of problems with that car. It would stall out. I'd pull over and start up again. Trucks were roaring past me. I'd get up to the top of a hill and start coasting down, and I'd think, Now I've got it made. The engine would run a little bit, but when I would put a drag on the engine, it would stall again.

It took me forty-five minutes to get from my house to the Shelbyville exit, ten miles away, where I limped off the expressway. I got to a telephone and called the minister of youth from the church where I was pastor; he was going to be in the class. I said, "Charlie, if you want to pass that class this semester, you'd better come pick me up."

Now, I'd known I could have problems with that car. I mean, when you get into a car, you know you can have problems with the car. And with a '77 Gremlin you can almost bet you're going to have problems with the car! Though I'd known it could happen, that didn't make it any easier to deal with when it did.

It still bothered me, and I prayed. I actually prayed, "God, I don't know why I'm having trouble! Don't you know where I'm going? I'm going to the seminary, God, to teach for you!"

It didn't make any difference. The car still didn't run. When crisis crashes in on our lives, no matter how ready we think we are, it always comes as a surprise. It never makes it any less difficult to deal with. It doesn't seem to help.

What was taking place frightened the disciples. Fear grabbed them. Notice what the text says. The storm came suddenly, and they didn't know what was going to happen. They didn't think it was too bad as the rain was coming down, but as the water began to fill the boat, they became frightened because they didn't know what was going to happen to them. When crisis comes in your life and in my life, I think the reason we get so frightened is the unknown. The unknown is so very frightening, because we *just don't know* what is going to happen.

My father passed away in April. My dad was a big man, six foot one or two, weighed two hundred and some pounds. I always looked up to him and was always amazed at what a pillar of strength he seemed. Six months before he died, they were going to do some tests, and I flew to Pennsylvania to be with him. When I got to the hospital, they were just wheeling him back from a lung biopsy. I went into his room; my stepmother was with him, and she stepped out of the room to talk to a nurse. I went over to my dad and took his hand, because I had never seen him so frightened before. I said, "Dad, what's the matter?"

He said, "I'm scared."

I said, "What are you scared of?"

He said, "I'm scared because I don't know."

That's right. The unknown is terribly frightening.

And it doesn't have to be a really big "unknown" like tests for cancer or other diseases. When my family moved from

Frankfort to Louisville, our children were scared when they had to go to a new school. The unknown is always frightening. It's just not knowing what it is going to be like.

Do you remember the first time you went to a dentist and saw all that stuff around the room? You didn't know what was going to happen. I went to an eye doctor when I was in the first grade, and I was scared to death. When I sat down and he brought an instrument over near my face, I opened my mouth. I didn't know what it was. I thought I was at the dentist's. I didn't know. It was frightening, because the unknown is always scary, always frightening.

We usually expect the worst. I think that's why churches have such difficult times making changes and going on into some new things, because the familiar is comfortable and we are happy. We don't have to worry about what we know, but when we try to do something different, it is scary.

That's what the disciples were facing. They didn't know what was going to happen to them. The suddenness of it, the fear— and then what comes is despair. Notice that they were not despairing because their ship was sinking. That is something to despair about. But, the despair that they had came because it seemed as though God didn't care. Look at verse 38: "Teacher, don't you care that we are perishing? Don't you care that we are drowning?" I think that's why we despair when illness comes to a loved one, when problems come, when death comes, when financial crisis comes. That's where the real despair is. We despair because of the problem; we lose hope because God doesn't seem to care. "Why don't you curse God and die?" Job's wife said. "God doesn't care. You've lost everything, Job. Why don't you curse God and die? He doesn't care about you. Can't you see that?" That's how the disciples felt. They just couldn't believe it. The ship was sinking around them, and Jesus didn't seem to care.

I think if you were to characterize the crises that you and I face year in and year out, perhaps month in and month out, we realize crisis has these characteristics: a sudden onset, though we may be prepared for it; the sudden onset brings anger and fear; anger and fear turn into despair. There's not much good news here, is there? But make sure you catch the rest of the story.

There is one thing we often miss in the text. Do you know what it is? *Jesus was in the boat.* That's right! He was in the boat. He wasn't on the shore. He wasn't over there on the bank watching. He wasn't out someplace keeping an eye on the boat from a distance. Jesus was in the middle of it, right in the middle of it!

They woke Jesus, and he looked out and spoke to the storm and quieted the wind. Then he turned to his disciples and said, "Why are you so afraid? Do you still not have faith?"

I hate it when he asks those kinds of questions. He always seems to ask them. You know what he was saying: "Did you really think that this boat would sink with me in it? Did you really think that? What's the matter with you?" Oh, I find it so easy to identify with the disciples: "Sure he's in the boat, but he's asleep!"

What do you do when you find Jesus asleep? Maybe he wants to know if we will respond out of faith.

The disciples were struck with awe. They wanted to know where all this power was coming from. First, he had power in the beginning of the Gospel of Mark to heal and cast out demons, to heal those who were sick, and now he speaks and nature itself listens to him. And at the end of the text, the disciples seem to say, "Who is this sleeping Savior?"

What do you do when you find Jesus asleep? Perhaps the Bible is saying, "Have faith and know he is in the boat with you, and there is no reason to fear or despair." Well, having faith while you're in a sinking boat with a sleeping Jesus is not easy; but it's possible.

Do you remember what the mother said when she found out little Karen had died? "Where is God when you need him?" I didn't tell you the rest.

She sat there, feeling that life was all over. Then she thought back four years earlier to another crisis. She and her husband had been married for six years, and they desperately wanted children. They were told they would probably not have any because she had RH-negative blood, but in the darkness of that prognosis she found out she was pregnant. She gave birth to a son.

In this moment of darkness, having just found out that Karen had died, the mother thought back on how God had been with her and her husband four years earlier, and though she couldn't feel his presence right then, though he seemed to be asleep right then, she realized that he was still there. The storm would soon be over.

She said she never could have made it through that difficult time had it not been for her faith in God. So having faith while in a sinking boat with a sleeping Jesus is not easy, but I know it is possible. Because I saw my mother weather the storm over the death of my baby sister, Karen; because she knew that God, who had been there before, was still there.

What do you do when you find Jesus asleep? Rejoice in the fact that he's in the boat, and claim the faith that he has the power to help you weather every storm. "I will never leave thee, nor forsake thee."

Reflection

Every congregation has members who are dealing with grief, sickness, the loss of work and the pain of divorce. These and other common issues always provoke the question, Where is God in the difficulties of life? The sermon was my attempt to respond to that question.

I began the sermon with a personal interest story, to create interest and to set the stage for the conclusion of the sermon. People would rather listen to stories about people than lectures about ideas. The bookend technique of beginning the sermon with my parents' story and ending with the story's conclusion was an intentional strategy of attitude. I did not want the congregation to know, too soon, that I was emotionally involved in the story; I wanted to lead them to that conclusion.

The concerns I list—the patient diagnosed with cancer, the family facing a layoff, the death of a loved one—are exemplary and not exhaustive. I repeated them and expanded the list intentionally to try to identify with most of my hearers. I repeated the rhetorical question "What do you do when you find Jesus asleep?" as a strategy to maintain unity and to keep the hearers involved in the sermon. The use of rhetorical questions is an excellent way to create a sense of dialog in a sermon.

The basic form I used was to follow the flow of the text—the calm before the storm; the storm; the disciples' panic; Jesus' calming of the storm; Jesus' questioning of the disciples; the disciples' struggle with who Jesus is. Movement was naturally created as the story unfolded before the hearers. I also hoped the hearers found their story in the sermon's story.

I illustrated the sermon with events from my life with which the congregation could identify. People often experience car trouble when they are in a hurry to get somewhere. Everyone has been frightened when faced with an unknown situation. We often wonder where God is during the difficulties of life. I try to show that I identify with the feelings and frustrations that they have during those moments. As their preacher, I do not live an insulated life. Through identification, I try to show them that I recognize their pains and hurts, and I search for God in crisis moments too. My goal for the congregation was that, having heard the sermon, they would know God's presence, no matter the circumstances—a realization that is difficult at times, but possible.

Worry-Warts[1]
Matthew 6:25-34

One of my students, Amy Jacks Dean, preached this sermon. Amy, a graduate of the Southern Baptist Theological Seminary in Louisville, Kentucky, is minister to students at First Baptist Church in Clemson, South Carolina. She preached this sermon to a different church, although the setting was similar. The congregation was predominantly professional—medical doctors, attorneys and businesspeople. There were many students present in the service. As a student herself, Amy knew what pressure students felt. When she began to think about her responsibilities and the concerns she heard from the students in the congregation, she became overwhelmed. They told her their worries; then she started to worry. The sermon developed as a response to her worrying about worry.

We had been married a little over three years when my in-laws (all eight of them) came to our place for Thanksgiving. I was a wreck trying to make sure everything was "perfect." The turkey was beautiful. I had casseroles of every color imaginable—yellow squash, green broccoli, orange sweet potatoes. We also had a red cranberry salad. It was a colorful table. I had also baked a pumpkin cheesecake. I was so worried about this meal because my in-laws are such wonderful people, not to mention wonderful cooks! I wanted everything to go smoothly and taste good. I was so worried that I was a nervous wreck and almost sick.

When it came time to eat, two children were trying to go to sleep, so their parents were lying down with them. We ended up eating in shifts and never blessed the food together. An unblessed Thanksgiving meal—can you imagine that?

All my worry had been for nothing. Everything did not go smoothly by my definition, but the worrying didn't do a thing to help. It was wasted energy.

Does anyone else here worry? I know I must be the world's worst worry-wart! I worry about money, security, jobs, family, traffic, others' feelings, school, parents, *everything!* Name someone that doesn't worry. Homeless people worry about where their next meal is coming from. I sometimes worry if I have enough starch and green vegetables for a balanced meal.

The point is not whether one worry is more valid than another; the point is that we all worry. Yet in the Gospel of Matthew, Jesus tells us not to worry. (Read Matthew 6:25-34 NIV.)

You know, I really don't like this passage of Scripture. I can remember hearing that if you had enough faith and prayed hard enough, God would provide, especially to ministers. When my husband and I decided to marry, my only stipulation was, "I cannot live under the condition that if we need more money, I will pray and then go to my mailbox and expect some nice person to have sent us money." Yet I read this passage from Matthew, and here Jesus is telling me not to worry. I find comfort in knowing that I don't have to worry or be anxious; yet some things about this passage are unsettling.

I came to the conclusion that verse 33 is the focal point: "But seek first his kingdom and his righteousness, and all these things will be given to you as well" (NIV). I had an even better understanding after reading this verse in the Revised English Version: "Set your mind on God's kingdom and his justice before everything else, and all the rest will come to you as well." It seems to be a matter of prioritizing what we are to be concerned or worried about.

First, before we can understand these verses, we need to make a distinction between our needs and our wants. Jesus is clearly telling us that God will meet our essential needs. Food and clothing should not be what we worry about. We should concern ourselves with God's kingdom and God's righteousness. God provides the food to maintain life and clothing to cover our bodies.

But where is God in the lives of so many starving people, people with no clothing or shelter? There are people like that all around us. How can we ask those people to seek God's kingdom and God's righteousness when their stomachs are growling and their teeth are chattering so loudly that it drowns out all our words about God? I would love to say, "Let's save that question for another sermon," but that would not be fair to this text.

Read verse 33 for yourself. If "all these things" (food and clothing—the essentials) have been given to you, then perhaps a portion of discovering the kingdom of God is in providing these essentials to those who do not have them. This passage tells us that we need not worry about those things. If we help everyone attain the basic physical needs discussed in this passage, maybe then they could stop worrying about being cold or hungry. They could then begin to think about seeking the kingdom and righteousness of God. Perhaps we leave too much in the hands of God and do not take enough responsibility in giving God a hand.

Yet we still hear Jesus' haunting words to us, "Don't worry." Even the popular singer Bobby McFerrin says, "Don't worry, be happy." I would love to take these words as they are, no questions asked, but I cannot do that. I am the kind of worry-wart that worries about if I am worrying about if I am worrying. Jesus said, "Don't worry," but I do!

But is it possible that Jesus was not saying, "Don't worry, period"? Jesus was fully human, and part of being human is that we worry. Do you think Jesus worried? Look at Matthew 26:36-38: "Then Jesus went with his disciples to a place called Gethsemane, and he said to them, 'Sit here while I go over there and pray.' He took Peter and the two sons of Zebedee along with him, and he began to be sorrowful and troubled. Then he said to them, 'My soul is overwhelmed with sorrow to the point of death. Stay here and keep watch with me' " (NIV). I hear worry in Jesus' statement.

I work in a hospital as a chaplain. When patients or family members are awaiting test results, or are waiting for a six-hour surgery to be completed, or a mother has gone into labor, worry happens. I do not say to them, "Jesus tells us not to worry." I can't say this to them, because I think Jesus himself did worry. It is interesting to me that Jesus wanted his disciples to stay with him. That is just what these people in the hospital want—someone to be there, to care, to stay with them.

I was on call the other day when a pastor of forty-six years wanted to see a chaplain. He had to make a decision that day about whether to put a feeding tube in his comatose wife to prolong her life. This decision worried him. He said, "I have prayed all night long about this, and I just don't feel any answer. I don't know what to do. I am trying to seek what God wants me to do, but I haven't figured it out yet. What do you think I should do?"

What a question! I didn't know what to say. After a few minutes, I said, "I can't tell you what to do, but I know this must be a terrible decision for you to have to make. I don't think there is a wrong decision."

This elderly pastor was worried, but he was seeking God in all of it. I think that's what Jesus did, and I think that's what he wants us to do.

When Jesus says, "Don't worry," he follows up with, "But seek . . ." Jesus does not say that in the seeking there will be no worrying. In fact, Jesus concludes, "Each day has enough trouble of its own," which says to me that he realizes that in seeking God's kingdom and righteousness there will be worries. I believe that God worries with us through those times.

Perhaps Jesus talked about worry so that worry would not consume us. Glenn Hinson, a professor I studied with in seminary, says, "Frustrated desires gone out of control result in jealousy, rage, murder, and all-out fighting to get what one wants. This is precisely the reason Jesus warned against worry."

Maybe Jesus wanted to warn us not to be consumed by worry, especially concerning food and clothing. He wanted us to seek God. When we seek God, with our worries and all, God will be there with us. There is some real comfort here because God knows about worry.

A great youth-retreat-campfire-sing-along-tear-jerker is the song "Seek Ye First." The lyrics are the words of verse 33 with one addition: "Seek ye first the kingdom of God, and his righteousness. And all these things shall be added unto you. Hallelujah." Let us say Hallelujah to the seeking, and to the worrying, and keep our sights set on God. Amen.

But There Are Giants in the Land
Numbers 13:25—14:4

Prospective students from colleges and universities throughout the United States come to Southern Seminary annually, in the fall and spring, to visit the campus and get a feel for seminary life. Most of them are nearing graduation and deciding where to pursue ministerial training. I preached this sermon in seminary chapel as a part of the preview conference. About 120 prospective students were present, with the regular student body and faculty.

"We've got some good news and some bad news," said the twelve spies to Moses when they returned from their expedition.

"Give me the good news first," Moses must have responded.

"The good news is the land to which you sent us is beyond our wildest dreams. It's an abundantly rich land," reported one of the scouts.

Another chimed in, "It makes this wilderness look like a—"

"Like a wilderness!" exclaimed still another. "The land is productive and luscious with fruit—grapes and pomegranates and figs." The fruit was a treat for those who had quickly grown tired of the heavenly provision of mueslix and Southern-fried quail.

"But the bad news is that the people who live in the land are very strong, and the towns are extremely large and well defended, and there are very tall people living there."

The twelve spies began to discuss and argue among themselves about what they had indeed seen. One of them, named Caleb, quieted them and said, "Let's go immediately and take the land and make claim to God's promise to us; we are clearly able to overcome it."

In the face of such a challenge, reality set in, and they got cold feet. All but Caleb and Joshua argued back: "We're no match for those people; they are much stronger than we."

While the spies were arguing among themselves, the Israelites impatiently waited to hear the report about the land. Like anxious children on Christmas Eve, they couldn't wait to receive their Promised Land. You can imagine their astonishment when they were told that all they would get this year is "coal in their stockings." The spies said to them, "We've got some bad news and some more bad news. The land we went through—our Promised Land—devours the people who live in it. It's an evil land. The people we saw there are gigantic; we seemed like grasshoppers next to them!"

And so the story unfolds. I sure would like to avoid stories like this one in the Bible—especially in the Bible. I like to believe that the Bible is a book full of faith stories, hero stories, stories about winners. But that's the problem with the Bible. The picture it paints is too real, too telling, too embarrassing. We cannot hide behind the stories of faith and heroes and winners, because standing right next to them are the stories of doubt and ordinary people and failures, all a part of the human-divine story.

The stories contained in the books from Exodus to Joshua are stories about a pilgrim people, a people on the move from bondage to freedom from a nightmare to making dreams a reality. Because it is a book about pilgrims on the way, is it possible that it is hauntingly our story too?

This story in Numbers reminds us that we, the church, are on a pilgrimage toward the goal of God's high calling in Jesus Christ—being God's covenant people in the world. That goal is filled with fruitful potential.

Jesus understood his ministry as bringing good news to the poor, proclaiming release to the captives and recovery of sight to the blind, letting the oppressed go free and proclaiming the year of the Lord's favor. Our call is to continue what Christ began, participating in making the gospel a reality. That's the fruit of the land.

We envision a world in which children will not cry themselves to sleep because they are hungry. We envision a world where children will be allowed to be children. Alex Kotlowitz wrote a book about the toll that inner-city violence takes on the children who live there. The book, *There Are No Children Here,* is the story of two brothers, Lafayette and Pharaoh Rivers, who live in Chicago's Henry Horner Homes, a public housing complex marred by crime and neglect. When the author approached their mother, LaJoe, he said he wanted to write about Lafayette and Pharaoh and the other children in the neighborhood. She liked the idea, then hesitated and said, "But you know, there are no children here. They've seen too much to be children."[2]

We envision cities where people will not have to sleep over steam grates to be protected from the bitter winter winds. We envision a time when illicit drugs will no longer capture the minds and bodies of our young people. We envision a time when senior adults will not be devastated by the oppression of astronomical health-care costs. We envision a place where people are more important than possessions. We envision telling the world that God gave Jesus Christ "so that everyone who believes in him may not perish but may have eternal life."

The Israelites brought grapes and pomegranates and figs to show the fruitfulness of the land. Some fruit for us is the joy of serving God, the satisfaction of participating in the gospel, the realization that salvation is not a foggy vision of a future hope but a real possibility for living now.

Some people say, "But there are giants in the land! The obstacles are too great, the work is too hard, the barriers too difficult to overcome."

Caleb didn't argue about the presence of the obstacles. There are very real obstacles facing the church. A recent report on National Public Radio said that one in ten people in this country is on food stamps—the highest percentage ever. More people than ever before are one paycheck away from joining the ranks of the homeless. Homelessness is a reality, from Miami to San Francisco to Louisville. The immensity of the problem of ministering to the poor stands in the way of local churches' making any kind of intentional response. We hear Jesus' words "You always have the poor with you" as permission to avoid acting on their behalf: "They don't want to help themselves. Anybody who wants to work can work. They'd work if they weren't so lazy; it's easier to collect food stamps." In our theological blindness we fail to see that the true mandate for a gospel people is "Just as you did it to one of the least of these who are members of my family, you did it to me" (Mt 25:40).

The culture of which we are a part presents obstacles to the church's fulfilling its call. Life in the fast lane of the eighties was slow compared to the hectic pace of the nineties. I don't know why it is, but we always cram at least twenty-nine hours of things to do into a twenty-four-hour day. Life today is like playing a 33⅓ record on 78. (Do they still have records today?) Entertainment is movies to go, pizza at regular price four bucks, four bucks, four bucks, and "I want my MTV." A family meal is pulling up to the drive-in window and hearing a maniacal voice shout: "Two burgers and an order of fries, cha ching!" Where is there any time for God?

Consumerism is a hallmark of our culture. People even shop for churches today. They want a church that meets their specific needs: How will your church contribute to my well-being? What does your church have to offer my teenagers? Baby boomers look for what works, what is efficient, what will bring a return on their investment. And they want their "purchases" guaranteed. I heard of a man who sued a church for false advertising. He said he was told that if he tithed, God would bless him with more than he had given. That didn't happen, and so he was suing the church to get his tithe back.

The loss of confidence in ministers and the popular view of the church as an irrelevant, archaic institution offering nothing vital to a complicated world stand as barriers to effective ministry. The church adds to that perception by dreading and fearing change, and by not risking because of the prospect of failure. Failure is a real possibility when one is facing giants. Like the Israelites, we view obstacles as hindrances rather than as opportunities to exercise faith.

Many of you here for the preview conference are spying out this "promised land" called seminary. You're trying to decide if this is the place to which God is calling you to prepare for ministry. I hope you will discover some fruit this place has to offer: An administrative staff that will do their best to make your transition to this place as painless as possible. A rich and diverse faculty—rich is not the right word—a faculty of depth, who are called and committed to the church and to classroom ministry. A theological library second to none in the world, housing the resources you will use as you pursue theological inquiry. A health and recreation center that has become the heart of the place, where we fellowship and play together—students, staff, faculty, families all paying the price for enjoying Baptist fellowship meals too much. The "land" here at Southern is rich and good and productive and fruitful.

But be warned—there are giants in the land. The financial pressures on students is very real and can be extremely discouraging. You will learn to do without things you once took for granted. There will be times when going out on the town is a McDonald's "Happy Meal" and a dollar movie.

You will work harder than you ever thought you could. Juggling schoolwork and church work and a secular job is not part of the curriculum, but you will learn to do it well.

Finding a place to live; finding work; if you have a spouse, finding a job for him or her; your children's need to make sense out of a new environment, new schools, new friends—these are all giants that will try to convince you that the move to seminary is too hard, that "the land is evil and we are not able to overcome it."

Your families back home will wonder why you're following God's call to this distant land. I like Fred Craddock's question: "Why is it that God never calls anyone into the ministry loud enough for their whole family to hear?"

Someone may have told you, "Don't go to Southern Seminary. There are giants in the land—liberals, you know!" I was told, "If you go to *that* school, they'll ruin you!" You may have been told that this place "devours its inhabitants."

You will be challenged here; you will be stretched here; the faculty will say things you don't always want to hear but need to hear; you will grow here; but you will not be devoured here.

Some of you will be graduating from seminary soon. You were prospective students once. You came here and challenged the obstacles in pursuit of your call to ministry. Now you're getting ready to leave what Tom Long calls "clergyland" and enter the *real* world of full-time ministry. The fruits are promising—a salary that may take you beyond the poverty level; a chance to put into practice what you learned here in theory. You'll be able to preach and not be criticized by your congregation; they won't say anything negative about your sermons as we did in preaching class.

But be warned—there are giants in the land. You are going out to minister in a world characterized by change more than ever before. The church doesn't like change, and you are called to lead the church, kicking and screaming, into the twenty-first century.

There are giants in the land; some churches devour their ministers. They have unrealistic expectations. Believing you can walk on water and raise the dead is not out of the question. Churches will take every moment of time you offer them and more. If you are willing to work a fifty-hour week, they will expect sixty. You will be tempted to meet all their expectations to the neglect of your welfare and the welfare of your family. Many ministers' children hate the church because the church robbed them of a parent.

You may be facing the giant of going to a new geographical location. "I'll go anywhere but New Jersey," said the student from Macon, Georgia, who was called to Hoboken . . . New Jersey. "I don't know anything about New Jersey. That's an evil land that devours its inhabitants. It's filled with giants—and not the New York type. I cannot overcome them."

Some of you are facing the giant of being refused the opportunity to exercise God's call because of who you are. For women in ministry, for divorced ministers, for ministers challenging the traditional way of doing things, the giants of narrow-mindedness and myopic theology stand in your way.

Caleb said, "Let's go up now and occupy the land, for we're well able to overcome it." But the spies gave a negative report: "The land devours its inhabitants. It is full of giants."

So the Israelites called a business meeting: "Would that we had died in the land of Egypt! Or would that we had died in this wilderness! Why is the LORD bringing us into this land to fall by the sword?" A motion was made and seconded: "Let us choose a captain, and go back to Egypt." The motion carried.

There is a real problem here—the matter of theology by majority vote. Ask Martin Luther or John Huss or Joan of Arc. Remember, it was the majority that crucified Jesus.

The Israelites spent forty more years wandering the wilderness because of their decision. They finally made it to the Promised Land, but that wasn't exactly what God had in mind. When will we learn that the voice of the majority is seldom the voice of God?

Rosa Lee Parks was forty-two years old in 1955. She was a seamstress who rode the bus to work every day in Montgomery, Alabama. She was an African-American. She had taken a seat in the front of the bus. A white passenger boarded the bus. The bus driver demanded that Rosa Parks move to the back of the bus where she "belonged" so that the white passenger could sit down. Rosa Parks refused to move. The police arrested her for violating a city law requiring African-Americans to sit at the back of the bus.

To protest her arrest, African-Americans staged a year-long boycott of the Montgomery bus system. That boycott, led by Martin Luther King, Jr., led to mass protests demanding civil rights for African-Americans.

Rosa Lee Parks was saying, "I'll face these giants, but I'll return to Egypt no more." She faced the giants of bigotry and ignorance and stereotypes and hatred.

She was not afraid of the giants in the land, because she took God's promises seriously: "I'll never leave you nor forsake you"; "I have come that [you] might have life, and have it more abundantly."

She took seriously the words she heard preached in church: "For freedom Christ has set us free. Stand firm, therefore, and do not submit again to a yoke of slavery" (Gal 5:1).

She took seriously the words she learned in school: "We hold these truths to be self-evident, that all [people] are created equal, endowed by their Creator with certain inalienable rights; that among these are life, liberty and the pursuit of happiness."

Rosa Parks knew there is no life back in Egypt. There is no liberty back in Egypt. There is no happiness back in Egypt. "No, I'll not return to Egypt," said Rosa Parks, "I'll face the giants, because that's the promised land!"

Caleb said, "Let's go immediately and face the giants and take the land; we are clearly able to overcome it because God will go with us."

John Keating was the unorthodox new English literature professor at Welton Academy for Boys and one of the founders of the "Dead Poets Society."[3] On the first day of the semester, Keating gathered the class in front of a trophy case.

"O captain, my captain," he said, quoting a line from a Walt Whitman poem. "In this class you may call me Mr. Keating, or if you're slightly more daring, 'O captain, my captain.' "

Keating then asked a student named Pitts—which, he noted, was a rather unfortunate name—to read a poem to the group.

Pitts read the words, "Gather ye rosebuds while ye may / Old time is still a-flying; / And this same flower that smiles today / Tomorrow will be dying."

"Gather ye rosebuds while ye may," repeated Keating. "The Latin term for that sentiment is *carpe diem*—seize the day."

Keating asked the boys to draw closer to the photos in the trophy case: "Peruse some of the faces from the past. You've walked past them many times; I don't think you've really looked at them. They're not that different from you, are they? Same haircut—invincible just like you feel—they believe they're destined for great things, just like many of you—their eyes are full of hope just like you. Did they wait till it was too late to make from their lives even one iota of what they were capable? Because you see, gentlemen, these boys are now fertilizer for daffodils. But if you listen real close you can hear them whisper their legacy to you.

"Go ahead. Lean in. Listen. You hear it?"

Keating whispered, "Carpe . . . Hear it? Carpe . . . Carpe diem. Seize the day. Make your lives extraordinary."

Take a risk. That's what Caleb was saying to the Israelites: "Carpe diem. Let's go up at once. Seize the day." Is that what you hear this morning? Seize the day. Make your lives extraordinary.

Summing Up: Questions for Reflection

1. What strategy of attitude did the preacher take?

2. Did the preacher intentionally develop identification in the introduction to the sermon? How?

3. How did the preacher make the sermon interesting for his or her hearers?

4. What sources did the preacher use for illustrative material?

5. Did the preacher use his or her imagination effectively in creating identification?

6. What strategy of form did the preacher use?

7. How did the preacher maintain unity in the sermon?

8. How did the preacher create movement in the sermon?

9. Did the sermon's form serve the purpose of the sermon?

10. How did the preacher's language enhance or inhibit identification?

11. Can someone meet God as a result of hearing this sermon?

12. What would life be like if the hearers took the sermon seriously?

8/Can These Bones Live?

Identification & Sermon Delivery

> You persuade a man only insofar as you can talk his language by speech, gesture, tonality, order, image, attitude, idea, identifying your ways with his.
> KENNETH BURKE, *A RHETORIC OF MOTIVES*

A sermon is not a sermon until we preach it. Books of sermons abound. Journals like *Preaching* and *Pulpit Digest* devote much space to printed sermons. The previous chapter contained three sermons in print. But like the dry bones of Ezekiel 37, until life is breathed into them, sermons locked into the words of a page will never live.

I have obtained printed manuscripts, even transcripts, of sermons that I heard preached, moving sermons that challenged my faith and encouraged my life. When I went back and read the manuscript, I felt like Peggy Lee, asking, "Is that all there is?" Something was missing: the personal presence of a preacher. The warmth of the preacher's voice to communicate excitement, anxiety, joy and passion, the immediacy of a person sharing intimately with other persons, makes preaching a dynamic event. Sermons take on life when we deliver them.

Effective sermon delivery is a major consideration for identification in preaching.

Personal Presence

Every preaching textbook has a section, or at least a chapter, on sermon delivery. My concern is to focus on aspects of sermon delivery needed to enhance identification with your congregation.

Kenneth Burke insisted that one's entire body takes part in the communication process. He stated that "communication deals with the choice of gesture for the inducement of corresponding attitudes."[1] He saw a relationship between thought processes and the way speakers express and communicate thoughts.[2] Not only the words we use but also the way we use our voices and bodies while preaching reinforces or inhibits identification; we must be interested in the physical elements of preaching. Body posture and movement, eye contact, hand gestures, facial expressions, the use of the voice—tonality, pitch, volume, range and rate of speech—and the handling of notes are all part of the preaching moment. You should consider these physical elements as intentionally as you do the exegesis of the biblical text and the composition of the sermon.

When you stand up to preach, all eyes in the congregation are watching you. You are already communicating as you make your way to the pulpit or, if you do not use a pulpit, to where you will preach. Your physical presence tells the hearers something about the message they are about to hear.

A preacher who slouches behind the pulpit and fumbles around with notes communicates to me that what is about to take place is not important or relevant. Preaching is important. You spent hours studying the biblical text. You struggled to find the appropriate strategies to make your sermon dynamic and interesting. You worked hard to make the sermon relevant to the life situations of your congregation. With great anticipation, like a child who has brought home a report card with all A's, you cannot wait to share this week's sermon. Your physical presence should communicate that excitement.

Stand erect, look at the people and preach. It is not time for additional announcements about the annual "Breakfast for Missions" coming up next Saturday. And it is not time for a little stand-up comedy, as though Sunday-morning worship were a facsimile of "An Evening at the Improv." Some preachers attempt to be cute and clever, always telling a couple of jokes to warm up the congregation before they preach. Such antics are totally inappropriate for worship. If we take preaching seriously, perhaps our congregations will also.

There is room, of course, for appropriate use of humor in preaching. But humor, like all other elements of preaching, should be a servant to the purpose of the sermon. Sometimes our sermons begin with the reading of the biblical text. Sometimes the text is read as a part of the sermon or has been read earlier as a part of the liturgy. My point is, whenever you begin to preach, preach with intentionality and purpose.

Avoiding "Preacherisms"

As you preach, avoid stereotypical *preacherisms*. One of these is leaning on the pulpit. Some preachers grip the pulpit so tightly that it gives me the impression that if they let go, the pulpit would fly away. Leaning on the pulpit or grabbing it with white-knuckled fists communicates anger and readiness for confrontation. Is that what you really want to communicate? Such stances do not show that you have your congregation's best interests at heart—a crucial consideration for creating identification.

Another common preacherism is pointing the index finger at the congregation. When I was growing up, the only people who pointed at me that way were people who were mad at me. When my mother was angry because of something I had done, she pointed her finger and scolded me for being bad. Teachers in school pointed their fingers when the class was unruly and disruptive. When a preacher points his or her finger at me, I become defensive and angry; I do not appreciate talking down and scolding from the pulpit. Pointing the index finger is a condescending gesture that does not foster identification.

Again, if you want to create identification with the congregation, avoid the *preacher voice*. Some preachers amaze me with the unbelievable metamorphosis that happens to their voices when they preach. Artificially deepening the voice to create a feeling of piety is as transparent as Saran Wrap. Where did we learn that preachers need to sound like James Earl Jones (the voice of Darth Vader) to preach effectively?

Disguising your voice and trying to sound like a great orator will fool only yourself. Identification means relating to the people where they are and where they know you are. Speak to them with the same voice you use when you pray with them around the fellowship table, when you visit them in the hospital, when you counsel with them in your study. Your natural voice comforts them in crisis; use the same voice to create depth, passion and identification in your sermon.

The final preacherism I will mention, though I know you have thought of others, is bouncing on the balls of one's feet to emphasize major parts of the sermon. Perhaps there is nothing offensive or harmful in this gesture—but it makes you look like all the other preachers who bounce on the balls of their feet for emphasis. In other words, gestures and mannerisms that give you the aura of a stereotypical preacher violate the whole idea of identification. You are not a generic preacher; you are this congregation's preacher with a message for them as one with them. Be yourself and preach. The preachers who speak to me and my needs most effectively are those who capture my attention because they are not like every other preacher I have ever heard. Their messages are fresh. They are fresh. They have discovered the wonderful grace to be themselves in Christ.

Be Deliberate in Delivery

As you preach, remember that you are sharing a message of

vital importance to you and your listeners. In so doing, you must do some intentional planning about how you are going to deliver the sermon. When telling a story, you can create wonderful images with the words and gestures you use. Some preachers can do this extemporaneously; most of us must plan and prepare beforehand so that our words and gestures are appropriate to the occasion and communicate the point of the story.

Think about using facial expressions and body posture to emphasize emotions in the sermon. Your voice and body can express fear, anxiety, happiness, grief and many other emotions. When you plan for these before you preach the sermon, the congregation will not just hear the emotions, they will feel them with you— identification.

Delivery should be appropriate to the content of the sermon. Putting your hands in your pockets generally communicates calm and relaxation. Be sure that the content of the sermon at that point calls for a relaxed style. Talking with your hands in your pockets about the crucifixion of Jesus does not communicate clearly. The congregation will sense a major discrepancy between what you are saying and how you are saying it.

One theorist said, "Whatever I say with words I must also say with my body."[3] Communication is a complicated endeavor.

Planning sermon delivery does not mean that you must choreograph every word and movement ahead of time. Such a process would make preaching wooden and artificial. It does mean asking and answering questions about delivery. For example, if the sermon calls for excitement, ask, How can I show I am excited? Think about a child running into the house to tell Mom and Dad that the ice-cream truck is coming down the street: "The ice-cream truck! The ice-cream truck! Can I have some money?" That is excitement. Do you convince your hearers that you are as excited about the sermon as the child is about the ice cream? Increasing your rate of speech, using a higher tone of voice, raising your eyebrows, opening your eyes wide and involving your hands will communicate excitement.

If a part of the sermon is challenging, ask, How do I communicate the challenge? If a personal story is sad, ask, How can I express sadness while avoiding emotionalism? Thinking about these issues before you preach will make your sermons come alive. You will preach with passion and power; your hearers will identify with that.

Timing is a crucial aspect of sermon delivery. Some preachers have never thought about the importance of timing, and then they wonder why their hearers did not get the point. Skillful storytellers know when to speed up, when to slow down, when to build to a climax and, finally, when to provide resolution. They know that an incorrectly timed punch line can ruin a story. They also know that a punch line delivered correctly brings home the point immediately.

Remember Nathan's skillful timing in his sermon to David? Timing should be carefully thought out and planned ahead of time.

A key to timing in oral communication is the use of pauses. For example, if you want to emphasize a crucial idea, you might think about using a well-placed pause. We forget that we are introducing the congregation to material that we've been working on all week. We must give them time to absorb, to consider and to reflect during our sermons. Effective pauses are wonderful tools to give the congregation a chance to do that.

While preaching, remember: understanding in oral communication is always at the ear of the hearer. The fact that you are completely clear about what you mean does not mean you have communicated that meaning to your hearers. A colleague shared the following quotation: "I know you believe you understand what you think I said, but I'm not sure you realize that what you heard is not what I meant." Effective communication is a complex process. The key to effective preaching is for you to remember that preaching is a dynamic event that requires you to use effectively all your skills of communication: your voice, your gestures, your personality, your spirit, your total self.

Evaluating Your Delivery

The best way to analyze your preaching is to have your sermons videotaped. Your congregation probably has someone who owns a portable camcorder and would be glad to videotape sermons at your request.

I suggest that you wait at least a week before doing any critique of a particular sermon. This allows some distance from the event; you will be more objective in your evaluation. When you view the tape, look and listen for each of the following: the use of your voice; hand gestures; facial expressions; body movement and position. Ask yourself questions like these: Is my delivery at each point appropriate to the content of the sermon? Am I communicating to the congregation, or am I disconnected from them? Am I identifying with the congregation through my tone of voice and gestures? Have I developed distracting preacherisms?

You probably will find things you want to change completely and others you want to improve. Try working on changing or improving one thing at a time. If you attempt to stop leaning on the pulpit, preaching with your hand in your pocket and speaking too fast all in one sermon, you may get so hung up on techniques that your message suffers. But if you evaluate one sermon a month as I've described, you'll be surprised at how quickly you will enhance your preaching.

To Read or Not to Read

In a doctor of ministry seminar dealing with preaching, we asked several laypersons to come and talk to the gathered preachers about their expectations of preaching. One woman remarked: "I don't want a sermon read to me. If the preacher has to read to me, just give me the manuscript and I'll take it home and read it myself." The other laypeople on the panel agreed. Perhaps their tradition or denominational bias influenced their response. Yet their reply shows that the issue of reading or not reading a sermon is of concern for effective sermon delivery.

Experienced preachers at conferences and students in the classroom want to know what is the *best* way to preach: Should I take a full manuscript into the pulpit? Are extended notes allowed? What about one note card with just a couple of reminders? Is it better to use no notes at all? I know preachers who take a full manuscript into the pulpit and read every word and others who preach without a single note in front of them. They preach effectively and are excellent communicators. I also know some preachers who would bore a congregation no matter what method they used—from reading to a free delivery style. When it comes to identification, however, there is something to be said for preaching without notes.

My Personal Journey

I began preaching as a full manuscript preacher. Each week I slaved over my sermon manuscript, honing every jot and polishing every tittle. Sweating over the phrasing of every sentence and every twist of a phrase was a major part of my sermon preparation. I couldn't wait until Sunday so that I could go into the pulpit and wax eloquent as I delivered my masterpiece to the congregation. I was sure that the sermon would not have impact unless I said it exactly as I had written it down.

As enamored as I was with the sermon I had prayed about and written, and as passionately as I tried to deliver it, I found that the congregation's response was not what I thought it should be. How do you gauge a congregation's response? Empirically that's tough, but preachers do it intuitively. The expressions on people's faces, the nod of a head, a look of contemplation, the way they are sitting and the way they speak to you after the service are not scientific measurements, but they do say something about your hearers' response to sermons.

Intuitively, I sensed that I wasn't communicating the message I had composed. After some analysis and critique from a helpful mentor, I came to the conclusion that I had made the fatal mistake of creating something for the eye rather than for the ear.

A sermon is something that is heard, not read. Preaching is an event created, not a document delivered. With these ideas in mind, I began to rethink my sermon-composition strategy. Clyde Fant's discussion of the oral manuscript was extremely helpful in cultivating my thinking.[4] I watched and heard several models who preached without notes. I moved from reading a full manuscript in the pulpit to preaching with extended note cards to preaching without notes.

The responses I began to receive, more explicit now than intuitive, convinced me that I was communicating more effectively with the congregation. My preaching had moved from reading a printed page to being in dialog with my hearers.

Dwight Stevenson and Charles Diehl write that preachers must be aware of their hearers "not in a general or confused way, but sharply enough to be able to observe and respond to their changing reactions, and to talk with them as individuals."[5] I found that when I was reading a sermon, I was unable to spark that kind of intimate communication.

A free delivery style enables me to communicate personally with the congregation as I deliver my sermon. The sermon becomes an event that is happening now; the manuscript stands behind me (actually, it stays in my study) as a reminder of the work I've done in preparing the sermon. Identification is established because I am no longer giving my hearers a manuscript; I am communicating, as Phillips Brooks would say, the Truth through my personality.

Preaching Without Notes
Here is a sketch of my sermon-preparation method. I begin on Monday morning with a study of the text for Sunday's sermon. By Tuesday, I complete my exegetical study of the passage and begin to select sermon strategies, keeping in mind the needs and concerns of the congregation and the prayerful direction of the Holy Spirit. Wednesday, I consult several commentaries and evaluate my interpretation of the text in light of that study. I think of some appropriate illustrations that might shed light on the text or make the sermon interesting. On Thursday I sketch out a rough plan for the development of the sermon. I try to be creative and let my imagination run wild. I come up with many ideas I cannot use for this sermon and file them away for future contemplation.

Friday is the day I compose the sermon. The text has been on my mind all week. Events of the week, billboards I have read, newspapers I have seen, people I have met and prayers I have prayed have all influenced my thinking.

I write the sermon out as a full manuscript. I do this for several reasons. I want to save the work I've done. Writing out a manuscript slows down my thinking, helps me organize and clarify my thoughts and tests my way of saying some things. When I write the manuscript, however, it is a script for the ear and not for the eye. I like to say, "I talk the sermon onto the page." It is not a polished manuscript. Sometimes a transition is missing here and a complete thought is missing there. These will come by the time I preach on Sunday morning.

I look over the manuscript once on Saturday. I get up early Sunday morning and spend some time in meditation, preparing for the worship events of the day. I begin to think about the sermon. I read over the manuscript once or twice, perhaps memorizing an important phrase or the punch line to a crucial story. By this time, the manuscript is taking a back seat and an oral product emerges. I think of the sermon as blocks of *ideas* I want to communicate rather than words. I talk through the sermon several times in my head, but I try not to overprepare.

When I preach the sermon, I forgive myself if I forget an illustration I wanted to use or an idea I had hoped to convey. I believe that what I sacrifice in precision is more than made up for in communication. My preaching sounds like my normal way of talking, unlike the polished manuscripts of old, which sounded too refined and too perfect to be oral events.

As I preach, I intentionally try to identify with my hearers. I watch them, rather than notes or a manuscript, to find out whether what I am saying makes sense. If the congregation did not understand something I said, I can say it in other words to try to clarify the idea. I try to look at the entire congregation. I attempt to communicate to the children and youth who are present as well as the adults. I have found that preaching without notes enhances my sense that identification is taking place. In the preaching moment, I connect with my hearers.

Summing Up

Real identification means that you must find the method of sermon delivery that enhances your gifts and skills as a preacher to identify with your hearers. As you do, you are truly becoming one with them.

Notes

Chapter 1: What Is Identification?
[1]Henry H. Mitchell, *The Recovery of Preaching* (San Francisco: Harper & Row, 1977).

[2]Karl Barth, *The Preaching of the Gospel*, trans. B. E. Hooke (Philadelphia: Westminster Press, 1963), p. 54.

[3]Raymond Bailey, transcribed from the videotape *A Guide to Improving Your Preaching*, tape 2 (Nashville: Broadman, 1990).

[4]Phillips Brooks, *Lectures on Preaching* (New York: Dutton, 1877), p. 110.

[5]Kenneth Burke, *A Rhetoric of Motives* (1950; rpt. Berkeley: University of California Press, 1969), p. xiv.

[6]Ibid., p. 55.

[7]Ibid. Kenneth Burke's writings and the writings of other early scholars do not reflect a sensitivity to inclusive language. I present quoted material as the authors wrote it in order to maintain the sense and tone in which it was originally written. However, I have attempted to be inclusive in my own writing.

[8]See Burke, *Rhetoric of Motives*, pp. 22-25.

Chapter 2: Identification & Preaching
[1]These characteristics were suggested by Donald Byker and Loren J. Anderson, *Communication as Identification: An Introductory View* (New

York: Harper & Row, 1975), p. 15.

²Fred B. Craddock, *Preaching* (Nashville: Abingdon, 1985).

³Ibid., p. 95.

Chapter 3: God with Us

¹See Raymond Bailey, *Jesus the Preacher* (Nashville: Broadman, 1990), and *Paul the Preacher* (Nashville: Broadman, 1991).

²Thomas G. Long, *Preaching and the Literary Forms of the Bible* (Philadelphia: Fortress, 1989).

³Other examples of Moses' intercession on behalf of the people include Numbers 9:1-14, specifically verses 6-8, and Numbers 11:1-3.

⁴Henry H. Mitchell, *The Recovery of Preaching* (New York: Harper & Row, 1977), p. 5.

Chapter 4: Taking Stock of Yourself

¹Brooks, *Lectures on Preaching*, p. 8.

²Tony Campolo, *The Kingdom of God Is a Party* (Waco, Tex.: Word, 1991).

³John Dever, "Quality in Southern Baptist Pastoral Ministry: Summary and Conclusions, Phase II, Part 1 Research," Southern Baptist Theological Seminary, Louisville, Ky. (typescript). A project funded by the Lilly Endowment, Inc. Used by permission.

⁴See Burke's discussion of substance in *Rhetoric of Motives*.

⁵Dever, "Quality," p. 6.

⁶Ibid., p. 12.

⁷Ibid., p. 6.

Chapter 5: Taking Stock of Your Scene

¹Dever, "Quality," pp. 14-18.

²Kenneth Burke, *Permanence and Change: An Anatomy of Purpose*, 3d ed. (Berkeley: University of California Press, 1984), p. 183. For issues having to do with the rhetorical *scene*, see also Burke's *Rhetoric of Motives*.

³Kenneth Burke, *The Rhetoric of Religion: Studies in Logology* (1962; rpt. Berkeley: University of California Press, 1970), p. v.

⁴See Kenneth Burke's discussion of *scene* as the container for rhetorical acts in *A Grammar of Motives* (1945; rpt. Berkeley: University of

California Press, 1969).

[5]Burke, *Grammar of Motives,* p. 77.

[6]George Barna, *The Frog in the Kettle: What Christians Need to Know about Life in the Year 2000* (Ventura, Calif.: Regal, 1990), p. 99.

[7]Barna's research group presents surveys on denominational decline in ibid., pp. 130ff.

[8]See Kenneth Burke's discussion of frames of acceptance and rejection throughout *Attitudes Toward History,* 3d ed. (Berkeley: University of California Press, 1984).

Chapter 6: Strategies for Identification

[1]Harry Emerson Fosdick, *The Living of These Days: An Autobiography* (New York: Harper & Brothers, 1956), p. 99.

[2]The story is my paraphrase of 2 Samuel 12:1-7, based on The Holy Bible, New International Version, 1973, 1978, 1984 by International Bible Society.

[3]See Clyde Reid, *The Empty Pulpit: A Study of Preaching as Communication* (New York: Harper & Row, 1967), pp. 25-33.

[4]Burke, *Permanence and Change,* p. 37.

[5]I highly recommend Lowry's work and often have students write sermons in class based on his homiletical plot: Eugene L. Lowry, *The Homiletical Plot: The Sermon as Narrative Art Form* (Atlanta: John Knox Press, 1980).

[6]Burke, *Permanence and Change,* p. 50.

[7]Raymond Bailey, "Proclamation as a Rhetorical Art," *Review and Expositor* 84 (1987), p. 17.

Chapter 7: Sample Sermons

[1]Amy Dean's sermon "Worry-Warts" is used by permission.

[2]Alex Kotlowitz, *There Are No Children Here* (New York: Doubleday, 1991), p. x.

[3]From the film directed by Peter Weir, *Dead Poets Society,* 1989.

Chapter 8: Can These Bones Live?

[1]Kenneth Burke, *The Philosophy of Literary Form: Studies in Symbolic Action,* 3d ed. (Berkeley: University of California Press, 1984), p. 281.

[2]Ibid., p. 130.

[3]Hans van der Geist, *Presence in the Pulpit: The Impact of Personality in Preaching,* trans. Douglas W. Stott (Atlanta: John Knox Press, 1982), p. 42.

[4]See the discussion about the oral manuscript and the sermon brief in Clyde Fant's *Preaching for Today,* rev. ed. (San Francisco: Harper & Row, 1987), pp. 165ff.

[5]Dwight E. Stevenson and Charles F. Diehl, *Reaching People from the Pulpit: A Guide to Effective Sermon Delivery* (1958; rpt. Grand Rapids, Mich.: Baker Book House, 1985), p. 98.

For Further Reading

Abbey, Merrill. *Communication in Pulpit and Parish*. Philadelphia: Westminster Press, 1973.

Achtemeier, Elizabeth. *Creative Preaching*. Nashville: Abingdon, 1980.

———. *Preaching About Family Relationships*. Philadelphia: Westminster Press, 1987.

———. *Preaching as Theology and Art*. Nashville: Abingdon, 1984.

Bailey, Raymond H., ed. *Hermeneutics for Preaching: Approaches to Contemporary Interpretation of Scripture*. Nashville: Broadman, 1993.

———. *Jesus the Preacher*. Nashville: Broadman, 1990.

———. *Paul the Preacher*. Nashville: Broadman, 1991.

Barth, Karl. *Homiletics*. Trans. Geoffrey W. Bromiley and Donald E. Daniels. Louisville, Ky.: Westminster/John Knox Press, 1991.

Bartow, Charles. *Effective Speech Communication in Leading Worship*. Nashville: Abingdon, 1988.

———. *The Preaching Moment: A Guide to Sermon Delivery*. Nashville: Abingdon, 1980.

Brueggemann, Walter. *Finally Comes the Poet: Daring Speech for Proclamation*. Philadelphia: Fortress, 1989.

Bugg, Charles. *Getting on Top When Life Gets You Down*. Nashville: Broadman, 1988.

Burghardt, Walter J. *Preaching: The Art and the Craft.* New York: Paulist, 1987.

Buttrick, David G. *Homiletic: Moves and Structures.* Philadelphia: Fortress, 1987.

Byker, Donald, and Loren J. Anderson. *Communication as Identification: An Introductory View.* New York: Harper & Row, 1975.

Chartier, Myron Raymond. *Preaching as Communication: An Interpersonal Perspective.* Nashville: Abingdon Press, 1981.

Cox, James W. *Preaching: A Comprehensive Approach to the Design and Delivery of Sermons.* San Francisco: Harper & Row, 1985.

Craddock, Fred B. *As One Without Authority: Essays on Inductive Preaching.* Enid, Okla.: Phillips University Press, 1980.

———. *Overhearing the Gospel.* Nashville: Abingdon, 1978.

———. *Preaching.* Nashville: Abingdon, 1985.

Davis, H. Grady. *Design for Preaching.* Philadelphia: Fortress, 1958.

Eslinger, Richard L. *New Hearing: Living Options in Homiletic Method.* Nashville: Abingdon, 1987.

Fant, Clyde E. *Preaching for Today.* Rev. ed. San Francisco: Harper & Row, 1987.

Fasol, Al. *A Guide to Self-Improvement in Sermon Delivery.* Grand Rapids, Mich.: Baker Book House, 1983.

Geist, Hans van der. *Presence in the Pulpit: The Impact of Personality in Preaching.* Trans. Douglas W. Stott. Atlanta: John Knox Press, 1982.

Gonzalez, Justo L., and Catherine G. Gonzalez. *Liberation Preaching: The Pulpit and the Oppressed.* Nashville: Abingdon, 1980.

Greidanus, Sidney. *The Modern Preacher and the Ancient Text: Interpreting and Preaching Biblical Literature.* Grand Rapids, Mich.: Eerdmans, 1988.

Lischer, Richard. *A Theology of Preaching.* Nashville: Abingdon, 1981.

———. *Theories of Preaching: Selected Readings in the Homiletical Tradition.* Durham, N.C.: Labyrinth Press, 1987.

Long, Thomas G. *Preaching and the Literary Forms of the Bible.* Philadelphia: Fortress, 1989.

———. *The Witness of Preaching.* Louisville, Ky.: Westminster/John Knox Press, 1989.

Lowry, Eugene. *The Homiletical Plot: The Sermon as Narrative Art Form.* Atlanta: John Knox Press, 1980.

McLaughlin, Raymond M. *The Ethics of Persuasive Preaching.* Grand Rapids, Mich.: Baker Book House, 1979.

Mitchell, Henry H. *The Recovery of Preaching.* San Francisco: Harper & Row, 1977.

Muehl, William. *Why Preach? Why Listen?* Philadelphia: Fortress, 1986.

Nichols, J. Randall. *Building the Word: The Dynamics of Communication and Preaching.* San Francisco: Harper & Row, 1980.

Noren, Carol M. *The Woman in the Pulpit.* Nashville: Abingdon, 1991.

Reid, Clyde. *The Empty Pulpit: A Study in Preaching as Communication.* New York: Harper & Row, 1967.

Ritschl, Dietrich. *A Theology of Proclamation.* Richmond, Va.: John Knox Press, 1960.

Rust, Eric C. *The Word and Words: Towards a Theology of Preaching.* Macon, Ga.: Mercer University Press, 1982.

Sider, Ronald J., and Michael A. King. *Preaching About Life in a Threatening World.* Philadelphia: Westminster Press, 1987.

Sleeth, Ronald E. *God's Word and Our Words: Basic Homiletics.* Atlanta: John Knox Press, 1986.

————. *Persuasive Preaching.* 1956; rpt. Berrien Springs, Mich.: Andrews University Press, 1981.

Troeger, Thomas J. *Creating Fresh Images for Preaching.* Valley Forge, Pa.: Judson Press, 1982.

Wardlaw, Don M., ed. *Preaching Biblically: Creating Sermons in the Shape of Scripture.* Philadelphia: Westminster Press, 1983.

Welsh, Clement. *Preaching in a New Key: Studies in the Psychology of Thinking and Learning.* Philadelphia: Pilgrim Press, 1974.

Willimon, William H. *Preaching About Conflict in the Local Church.* Philadelphia: Westminster Press, 1987.

Wilson, Paul Scott. *Imagination of the Heart: New Understandings in Preaching.* Nashville: Abingdon, 1988.